BestMasters

Springer awards „BestMasters“ to the best master’s theses which have been completed at renowned universities in Germany, Austria, and Switzerland.
The studies received highest marks and were recommended for publication by supervisors. They address current issues from various fields of research in natural sciences, psychology, technology, and economics.
The series addresses practitioners as well as scientists and, in particular, offers guidance for early stage researchers.

Vadim Kufenko

Economic Growth and Inequality

Empirical Analysis for the Russian Regions

Foreword by Prof. Dr. Harald Hagemann

Springer Gabler

Vadim Kufenko
Stuttgart, Germany

BestMasters
ISBN 978-3-658-08082-2 ISBN 978-3-658-08083-9 (eBook)
DOI 10.1007/978-3-658-08083-9

Library of Congress Control Number: 2014956683

Springer Gabler

Printed on acid-free paper

Springer Gabler is a brand of Springer Fachmedien Wiesbaden
Springer Fachmedien Wiesbaden is part of Springer Science+Business Media
(www.springer.com)

Foreword

The Master thesis of Vadim Kufenko is focused on the economic growth process in Russia since the early 1990s. Compared to other countries in transition, it is strongly dependent on natural resources. The main innovative merit of the thesis is the detailed and sophisticated empirical analysis of economic growth for the diverse regions of Russia. In Chapter 1 the author investigates different types of convergence and catching up for the regions; then, the cross-section and dynamic panel data methods are applied to estimate the determinants of growth and the speed of convergence. Chapter 2 consists of the game-theoretic analysis of the resource curse, which is extremely relevant for the Russian economy. Chapter 3 focuses on the relation between income and inequality. The estimation of the logistic models, based on the revolution constraints from the works of Acemoglu and Robinson, shows that specific measures of income inequality are a robust determinant of the risk of protests during 2011-2012. In general, the thesis of Vadim Kufenko investigates a number of relevant economic and political topics and represents an excellent synthesis of theoretical and empirical analysis.

Prof. Dr. Harald Hagemann
Stuttgart,
September 2014

Acknowledgements

This Master thesis has been written as a part of the research project on Social Capability, Economic Growth and Structural Change in Russia within the research network Institutions and Institutional Change in Postsocialism: Between History and Global Adaptation Pressures (KOMPOST) funded by the German Federal Ministry of Education and Research. The author would like to thank his parents, Anna Nabirukhina and Sergei Kufenko, for their support and Prof. Dr. Harald Hagemann for his remarkable guidance, enthusiasm, encouragements and help during the supervision of the thesis. The author would like to express his gratitude to the second supervisor Prof. Dr. Nadine Riedel, Prof. Dr. Robert Jung and his colleagues from the Department of Economics for their invaluable suggestions and ideas. The author is also grateful to Prof. Dr. Alexander Libman for his inspiring works and Dr. Constanze Dobler for her help in the past.

Vadim Kufenko
Stuttgart,
September 2014

Contents

Introduction ... 1

1 Economic Growth ... 4
1.1 Neo-classical growth model ... 4
1.2 Extensions of the neoclassical growth model ... 9
1.3 Literature overview: economic growth ... 13
1.3.1 Cross-section growth regressions ... 14
1.3.2 Dynamic panel data ... 17
1.4 Data ... 21
1.5 Empirical strategy and results ... 24
1.5.1 Estimation results: cross-section growth regressions ... 29
1.5.2 Estimation results: dynamic panel data ... 36
1.6 Summary of Chapter 1 ... 40

2 The resource curse and human capital ... 42
2.1 The resource curse: the Dutch disease and institutions ... 42
2.2 A game-theoretical approach to the brain-drain problem ... 52
2.3 Summary of Chapter 2 ... 60

3 Economic Growth and Income Distribution ... 62
3.1 Literature overview: economic growth and income distribution 63
3.2 Stylized facts on growth and distribution in Russia ... 72
3.3 Data ... 76
3.4 Empirical strategy, analysis of protests and results ... 78
3.5 Summary of Chapter 3 ... 85

4 Conclusion ... 87

References ... 93

List of Tables

1 Solow growth numerical simulation 7
2 Data for cross-section OLS growth regressions 21
3 Data for FD and two-step System GMM 24
4 Basic OLS growth regressions 32
5 Extended OLS growth regressions 34
6 FD and two-step system GMM 39

7 Specialization in fuels and high-tech goods 45
8 Sectoral structural change 45
9 Sub-sectoral structural change 46

10 Data for the logistic regression 77
11 Logit estimates of protest determinants (with Marginal Effects) 84

12 Tests for model (13.2), Chapter 1 105
13 Tests for model (13.3), Chapter 1 106
14 List of regions (Goskomstat order) 107

Introduction

The neo-classical growth model has withstood several waves of criticism and evolved from a relatively simple Solow model with exogenous variables into a more complex system with endogenously determined variables. Consisting of an intuitive production function of labour and physical capital which can be traced back to classical economists, and based on the neo-classical idea of diminishing returns to physical capital, the Solow model has turned out to be fruitful ground for several generations of researchers who not only introduced new variables to it (e.g. human capital), but also empirically tested its validity on the real data. The means of estimating the determinants of growth and convergence, which is one of the main implications of the neo-classical model, have also evolved: from OLS (further Ordinary Least Squares) cross-section growth regressions to one of the most sophisticated dynamic panel data estimation methods - the system GMM (further Generalized Method of Moments). Estimation tools have evolved, but that is not all. The attention of todays researchers is now drawn not only to the cross-country, but even to the regional dimension, which now allows scientists to take advantage of regional heterogeneity, typically lost during macroeconomic aggregation. Particular attention these days is also drawn to economies in transition since application of growth theory to industrialized market economies already represents common knowledge.

The topic of our research is economic growth and income distribution with empirical analysis for the Russian regions. We will try to focus specifically on growth, issues and biases to growth and income distribution and, in addition, link economic growth and income distribution. The goal of this research is to empirically identify and estimate the key determinants of economic growth for Russian regions, estimate convergence, discuss the main problems and threats to economic growth of Russia, build a bridge between economic growth and income inequality with the help of the politi-

1

Economic Growth

Bearing in mind the fact that this is an empirical work, in this chapter we will briefly discuss the context and the evolution of the neo-classical growth model in order to create sufficient theoretical foundation for the empirical models used in other sections.

1.1 Neo-classical growth model

Dynamics of key economic variables has been a fruitful topic of theoretical modeling for many economists long time before the well-established Solow growth model was published: for example Ramsey (1928, p.547) where the author formulated the optimal savings rate for capital accumulation considering marginal utility of consumption and marginal disutility of labour. Even though this work was focused on a specific aspect of capital accumulation, the optimal savings rate, it was very influential for the extensions of the Solow model which will be further considered in this chapter.

As mentioned in Hagemann (2009, p. 67), the roots of the modern dynamic growth theory can be found in the early works of Harrod. The main challenge seen by Harrod (1939, p. 15) was to "think dynamically" and to be able to trace long-run effects and interactions between variables. Obviously, a static apparatus is not fully capable of dealing with flow variables and their streams. In Harrod (1939, p. 16), the starting point of the analysis is the joint of the acceleration principle and the multiplier theory. The reason why we start with this very work of Harrod is that it illustrates the basics of the modern growth theory. These simple features can be still found in more sophisticated models. The acceleration principle is needed in order to derive values and solutions in time as well as for a continuous representation of a variable, whereas the multiplier theory describes an impact of an exogenous variable on the dependent variable. This impact or effect can be quantified by a certain coefficient. Thus, the merger of the acceleration principle and the multiplicator theory allows us to represent growth of variables of interest in time and analyze their determinants. The fundamental equation postulated by Harrod (1939, p. 18) states that if "the value of the increment of stock of capital per unit increment of output" is equal to "the amount of capital per unit increment of output required by technological or other conditions", then the actual change of these ratios would correspond to the change "justified by the circumstances". Therefore Harrod actually formulates a steady growth path since, according to him, under the latter condition the warranted growth of the output would be equal to the actual growth. The term "warranted" is distantly related to a certain understanding of equilibrium, since Harrod (1939, p. 16) explains this term as a situation where "all the parties are satisfied" and produce the "right" amount of output. Harrod perfectly fits his dynamic understanding to the ex ante and ex post dimensions used by Keynes as in Harrod (1939, p. 20), stating that deviations from the steady path may be related to discrepancies between ex ante and ex post variables. Thus, Harrod allows for policy interventions, for example as in the case when ex ante investments are greater than savings as in Harrod (1939, p. 19). In Harrod (1939, p. 23), the steady growth path is determined by the propensity to save and by the technologically required amount of capital per unit of output. The smallest departure from the path would induce further deviations making the system unstable. Later, Solow (1956, p. 65) calls this vulnerable equilibrium a "knife-edge" equilibrium. These two main features of the above-mentioned model stimulated scientific discussion and triggered further improvements to the modelling of the economic growth.

As we see, the main contribution of the above-mentioned work is merging the acceleration and multiplication on the way from static analysis to a dynamic one, defining the concept of a steady growth path and discussing the stability conditions. As in Hagemann (2009, p. 68), Harrod and consequently Harrod-Domar models can be related to the Keynsian tradition. A different prospective was offered by Tinbergen (1942) who, according to Hagemann (2009, p. 68), was the first to apply the Cobb-Douglas function to growth equations considering population growth, technical progress and capital formation.

The first works of Robert Solow, for example Solow (1952), were focused on various problems of dynamic equations: linking static and dynamic systems, stability conditions, persistence of oscillations and other issues. Solow (1953) is merely a criticism of the Harrod model and introduction of prices into the equations. However, Solow (1956) is a completely different paper: one of the main contributions of his paper was introduction of the growth model, which later was labeled as the Solow-Swan, for Swan (1956), model.

Solow (1956, p. 66) highlights the fact that his model is consistent with the Harrod-Domar model with two exceptions: the fixed-coefficients assumption and flexibility of factor prices. Solow (1956, p. 76) discusses the Cobb-Douglas function with capital and labour elasticity summing up to unity. The corresponding production and capital accumulation equations will become the foundation of many far more advanced models.

Let us consider the Cobb-Douglas production function for the basic Solow model as in Acemoglu (2009, pp. 36-37):

$$Y(t) = F\big(K(t), L(t), A(t)\big) = AK(t)^{\alpha}L(t)^{1-\alpha},\ s.t.\ 0 < \alpha < 1 \tag{1}$$

Where α is elasticity, $Y(t)$ is the output, $K(t)$ is the physical capital, $L(t)$ is labour and $A(t)$ is the efficiency parameter, which as we will discuss later, can be associated with technology or/and human capital. Dividing the equation by $L(t)$ we obtain the per capita function of the following form as in Acemoglu (2009, p. 37):

$$y(t) = Ak(t)^{\alpha} \tag{2}$$

Where $y(t)$ is output per capita and $k(t)$ is capital-labour ratio. The transitional dynamics of physical capital is determined by the following rule, as in Acemoglu (2009, p. 53):

$$\dot{k}(t) = sAk(t)^{\alpha} - \big(n + g + \delta\big)k(t) \tag{3}$$

Where $\dot{k}(t)$ is the change of physical capital in time, s is the savings rate applied to output (or the part of output to be invested), n is the growth rate of population, g is the technological change and δ is depreciation rate. Thus the steady state of the capital-labour ratio can be defined from Acemoglu (2009, pp. 53-55) as follows:

$$k^* = \left(\frac{sA}{n + g + \delta}\right)^{\frac{1}{1-\alpha}} \tag{4}$$

Let us conduct a MATLAB simulation to demonstrate the key properties of the Solow growth model. We will use the simple model for the simulation and discuss the extensions of it. The solutions to the differential equations will be obtained with the "ode45" command which is standard for dynamic optimization. Let us input the following values for specification (I) with a low starting point and (II) with a starting point at 50% of the steady state under the conditions as in the Table 1 below. For simplicity we assume no population growth and no technological change. Efficiency parameter is set to unity.

Table 1. Solow growth numerical simulation

Variable	Value (I)	Value (II)
$y_{t=0}$	0.001	3.7195
s	0.5	0.5
A	1	1
α	0.4	0.4
n	0	0
g	0	0
δ	0.15	0.15
periods	100	100

Data: proprietary

The steady state under conditions from Table 1 is 7.4381 in both cases, which is marked by the reference line linking 0 and the steady state; however, in (I) the initial income is 0.01% of the steady state, whereas in (II) the initial income is 50% of the steady state. We omit the case of 0 income at the starting point, since otherwise we will not have any savings since the savings are a fraction of output as well as consumption. Let us note that consumption in a steady state takes the following form as in Acemoglu (2009, pp. 37-39):

$$c^* = \left(1 - sf(k^*)\right) \tag{5}$$

In the framework of the neo-classical growth, investments are associated with savings, which are a fraction of the output. The flow of investments fosters physical capital accumulation, whereas consumption does not contribute to the physical capital stock. The consumption maximizing level of physical capital-labour is named "the golden level", and the "golden rule" of capital accumulation takes the following form as in Acemoglu (2009, p. 42):

$$f'(k_{gold})_{Solow} = \delta \tag{6}$$

We should highlight the key theoretical finding of the basic Solow model with physical capital: the growth rates are directly related to the distance between the steady state and the initial level. In other words, as in Sala-i-Martin (1994, pp. 743-744), "the growth rate of an economy" is "inversely related to the distance from its steady state". This theoretical finding is known as the β-convergence and as we will see from the empirical part of the given chapter, it is supported by empirical facts.

Let us assume that there exists a finite set of production functions, initial income levels and steady states. Each of the functions, initial levels and steady states are unique for each country or a region within a country. In this case, we would assume that with time the output of these countries or

Fig. 1. Simulation (I)

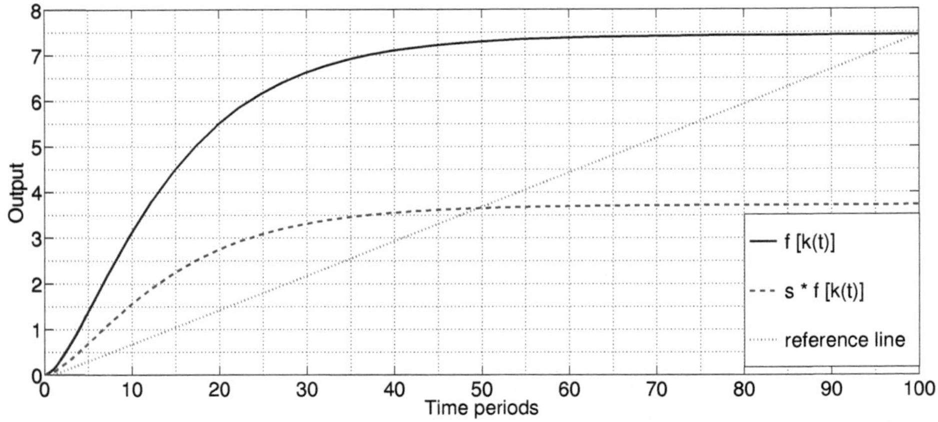

Source: proprietary numerical simulation

Fig. 2. Simulation (II)

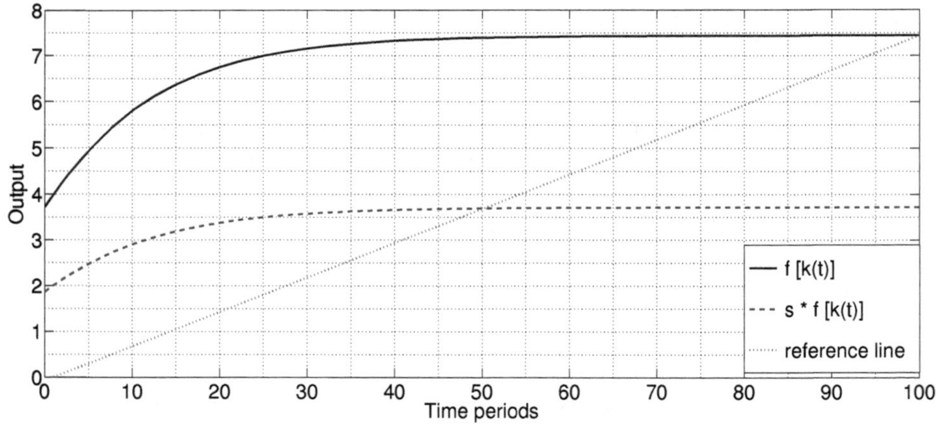

Source: proprietary numerical simulation

regions will converge to their unique steady states. As we observe from simulations (I) and (II), the growth rates decrease while the distance from the steady state decreases. Therefore, cross-country or cross-regional volatility of output would decrease, if the countries or regions are converging to their steady states. Young et al. (2008, p. 3) define the idea of σ-convergence as "a gradual decrease of dispersion and variation of income with time". β-convergence in Young et al. (2008, pp. 5-6) is discussed as a necessary but not a sufficient condition for σ-convergence. This finding can be traced back to Sala-i-Martin (1996, pp. 1327-1329). Based of the above-mentioned theoretical definition, we can state the following:

Proposition 1. *β-convergence is defined as an inverse relation between the growth rate and the distance from the steady state as in Sala-i-Martin (1994, pp. 743-744); whereas σ-convergence can be defined as "a gradual decrease of dispersion and variation of income with time" as in Young et al. (2008, p. 3).*

Bearing in mind the above-mentioned proposition, we have to state that β-convergence can be conditional on growth determinants. The unconditional convergence does not take these into account. One should note that in the first version of the Solow model only physical capital and labour entered the production function. The per capita adjustment transformed the function accordingly. The basic neoclassical growth model offers limited choice of variables to perform empirical analysis and thus we need to consider its extensions. As we have demonstrated, in the basic Solow model, economic growth is influenced by physical capital, labour, efficiency parameter, population growth rate, technological progress and depreciation.

In the above-mentioned basic version of the Solow model, growth of n, g and δ decreases the steady state, whereas s and A have a positive impact on the steady state level. As stated in Aghion and Howitt (2008, p. 29) technological change or growth of the efficiency parameter would offset the diminishing returns to capital: "the economy approaches a steady state in which the two conflicting forces of diminishing returns and technological progress exactly offset each other and the output/capital ratio is constant". Thus, technological progress is decisive for growth and performance.

We should note that the above-mentioned model is exogenous, whereas many of the extensions treated the key variables as endogenous, as in Romer (1994b, p. 3), determined within the system. Indeed, the necessity to extend the model can be seen from the empirical facts: as in Romer (1994b, pp. 4-10), the difference in growth rates and income variation among countries can be only partly explained by the basic model leaving a large residual. Later the term was coined as the "Solow residual", or the part of growth which cannot be explained by the variables from the basic Solow model.

The extensions deal with these and additional variables, which are included in the production function, and their endogenous nature.

1.2 Extensions of the neoclassical growth model

One of the first solid extensions was in fact the Ramsey-Cass-Koopmans (further RCK) model. Cass (1965) and Koopmans (1965) have based their work on Ramsey (1928) . In general, the Ramsey-Cass-Koopmans represents the Solow growth model with one significant difference: in this model the savings rate (s) is not exogenously given but rather is a product of household utility optimization problem. Namely, the RCK model adds household consumption dimension, which includes preferences, income flows and asset prices, to the growth model. As stated in Aghion and Howitt (1997, p. 19), the "golden rule" of capital accumulation in the given model takes the following form:

$$f'(k_{gold})_{RCK} = p + \delta \tag{7}$$

Where p is the "competitive rate of interest". In the RCK model p is equal to the ratio of income flow to the asset price. Other implications do not significantly differ from the original ones, previously mentioned in the basic Solow model including the convergence process. As we see, the RCK endorses endogenous treatment of the variables within the Solow growth model.

An interesting attempt to endogenize technology (A) and technological progress (g) was made by Arrow (1962, p. 155), who offered an "endogenous theory of knowledge". Arrow (1962, p. 156) argues that productivity growth can be observed even under relatively constant levels of physical capital. Thus, "learning by doing", as in Aghion and Howitt (1997, p. 22), and accumulating experience may be one of the reasons for a growing productivity other things equal. In Arrow (1962, p. 159), technological growth driven by "learning by doing" resolves the problem of diminishing returns to production factors since the "additional amount" of the given factors "can be used more efficiently". One may assume that experience is related to human capital; however in Arrow (1962, p. 157), "cumulative gross investments (cumulative production of capital goods)" are used as an index for experience which does not directly address the issues related to human capital.

The introduction of human capital into macroeconomics in general and into growth theory in particular has a relatively long history. Mincer (1958) focused his analysis on returns to schooling and education at a microeconomic level. His work has evolved into so-called "Mincer equation" and, as in Heckman et al. (2005, pp. 7-9), has become a solid framework for empirical analysis of returns to education. Becker (1975), being known for formulating the labour-leisure trade-off contribution to the neoclassical labour market theory, also contributed to empirics of return to education. One of the first statements on the positive relation of human capital (H) and economic growth can be found in Schultz (1961). Schultz (1961, pp. 4-7) states that investments in human capital may play a decisive role for growth. However, the first work to build a link between human capital and the Solow model was Uzawa (1965). Uzawa (1965, p. 19) relates technical progress, or g in terms of the original Solow (1956) model or $\frac{\dot{A}}{A}$ in terms of Uzawa (1965), to the share of labour employed in the educational sector. This was a very delicate way of including human capital into the model; however, until Lucas (1988) and Mankiw et al. (1992), human capital accumulation was not explicitly defined in the Solow growth model.

Another interesting example on the nexus of topics of technology and human capital was a Nelson and Phelps (1966), dealing with technology diffusion and adaptation. The pace of these processes, according to Nelson and Phelps (1966, p. 72), depends on the level of human capital:

$$A(t) = Tech\big(t - w(h)\big) \;\; with \;\; w'(h) < 0 \tag{8}$$

Where $w(h)$ is a time lag related to adoption of a new technology (assuming exogenous technological change) and dependent on human capital and $Tech$ is a theoretical level of technology. The lag decreases with an increase in human capital. Based mainly on Uzawa (1965), Lucas (1988, p. 19) has integrated human capital into the production function and proposed a human capital accumulation function, where the key ingredient is the effort to accumulate:

$$\dot{h}(t) = h(t)\psi\big(1 - u(t)\big) \tag{9}$$

Where $\dot{h}(t)$ is the change of human capital, ψ [2] is the human capital accumulation growth rate and $1-u(t)$ is an effort. If effort is equal to unity, then human capital grows at a full rate.

The main merit of Lucas (1988, p. 17-18) was not only a thorough integration of endogenous human capital into the neoclassical growth model, but also a distinction between internal and external effects of human capital. One should note that human capital externality in Lucas (1988, p. 18) enters the goods production function, whereas internal aspects associated with returns to education receive less attention.

Mankiw et al. (1992) is a blend of theory and empirics. The authors empirically test the impact of human capital on growth and augment the Solow model by adding human capital to the production function as in Mankiw et al. (1992, p. 416):

$$Y(t) = K(t)^{\alpha} H(t)^{\beta} \big(A(t)L(t)\big)^{1-\alpha-\beta}, \; s.t. \; \alpha + \beta < 1 \tag{10}$$

Where $H(t)$ denotes human capital. A small digression on the role of technology is necessary: one could assume a total factor productivity impact

[2] Notation deliberately changed from the original since the original one contradicts with δ used earlier for depreciation.

of technology $A(t)K(t)^{\alpha}L(t)^{1-\alpha}$, impact only on capital goods productivity $\left(A(t)K(t)\right)^{\alpha}$ and impact only on labour productivity $K(t)^{\alpha}\left(A(t)L(t)\right)^{1-\alpha}$, which is the case of Mankiw et al. (1992).

The per capita transformation in Mankiw et al. (1992) involves efficient labour, which means that both sides of equation are divided by $A(t)L(t)$. Therefore the human capital accumulation takes the following form as in Mankiw et al. (1992, p. 416):

$$\dot{h}(t) = s_h y(t) - (n + g + \delta)h(t) \tag{11}$$

Where s_h is a fraction of income invested in human capital. A small digression is necessary. Mankiw et al. (1992) for simplicity use the same notation for the depreciation rate for physical and human capital. One could assume there exists δ_h which is a specific depreciation rate for human capital. In Chapter 2 we will consider the brain-drain issue which could be related to the depreciation of the human capital. This would significantly complicate the set of accumulation and steady state equations.

The equation (11) literally tells us that human capital has its own saving rate. In addition, it may have its unique depreciation rate, if we assume, for example, the so-called brain-drain. In Chapter 2, we will focus on this problem and apply game-theoretic tools to this issue, specific for Russia. Once human capital enters the model, its level and the related savings rate also influence the steady states. In the empirical part of Chapter 1, we will include a proxy for human capital in our growth regressions; whereas Chapter 2 is focused on the resource curse and its impact on human capital. In Chapter 3, we discuss the Acemoglu and Robinson (2002) political Kuznets curve - a model, in which human capital along with unequal income distribution has a decisive impact on political developments and may even lead to a revolution. We should briefly note that we consider human capital to be one of the key determinants of growth which will be empirically shown with the help of growth regressions.

Last important aspect which fits into the neo-classical framework is institutions. As stated in North (1990, p. 137), "institutions" largely "determine the performance of economies". North (1990, pp. 131-136) discusses how an institutional matrix evolves historically by building up and adopting efficient and inefficient institutions. A very precise definition of institutions can be found in Aoki (2001, p. 26): "an institution is a self-sustaining system of shared beliefs about how the game is played". Naturally, under the term "game" one should understand a model of interaction between certain agents in various dimensions. Aoki (2001, pp. 47-50) finds game theory to be an elegant tool to show that institutions, whether formal or informal, may be established and self-sustained as an equilibrium outcome of a series of games. Whereas researchers like North (1990), Aoki (2001) and Hedlund

(2005) highlight the importance of history and informal proto-institutions (fundamental institutions, e.g., the rule of law or property rights), Acemoglu (2009, p. 853) suggests that formal and political institutions also play an important role since they impact on the distribution of resources, which may foster or hinder economic performance. Nevertheless, as stated in Acemoglu et al. (2001), historical aspects of formation of institutions, for example, the rule of law, are extremely important and can partially explain variations in income among countries. Hedlund (2005) conducts an impressive historical study of evolution of institutional matrix of Russia since the early middle ages to show path dependence, pointing out certain inefficient institutions, which create biases towards sustainable economic growth in Russia. Among these institutions, Hedlund (2005, pp. 26, 28, 36 and 43) mentions stationary bandits, weak property rights, patrimonial state and autocratic "Moscovy". Another interesting example of works on institutions is Hoff and Stiglitz (2004), where a game-theoretic model explains decision-making regarding building and stripping assets under a certain institutional environment and the emergence of the rule of law. One of the conclusions of Hoff and Stiglitz (2004, pp. 760-763) is that agents, which are stripping assets, will eventually stop and start promoting rule of law in order to protect and build assets. One should note, that Hoff and Stiglitz (2004) consider only one generation of asset-strippers (and other agents) and the model conclusions could be altered once we allow multiple generations, longer time horizons and uncertainties.

Proposition 2. *Saving, population, technology, depreciation, physical and human capital, informal and formal, e.g., political institutions, can be considered as key determinants of growth and output variation.*

There are numerous other extensions of the neoclassical growth model; however, we must keep in mind that this work is empirical. Let us proceed to discussing the existing literature of empirical analysis of growth.

1.3 Literature overview: economic growth

Tinbergen (1942) can be considered as one of the first statistical works on economic growth limited to Germany, France, the UK and the US during 1870-1914. One should note that modern literature involves more sophisticated empirical methodology and a broader country or region selection. Growth regressions estimated by the OLS represent a convenient and elegant way of estimating dynamic causal effects of determinants of economic growth in a static framework. A growth regression represents a linear relation between the growth rates during a certain period of time and initial values of growth determinants. This specification has certain advantages.

Firstly, we avoid endogeneity and reverse causality as in Wooldridge (2002, pp. 50-51), since the initial values of the growth determinants cannot be possibly influenced by the growth rates for the entire period. In other words, if we apply a simple cross-section regression for one year to regional data, we would have investments explaining economic growth; however, it is reasonable to assume that investments are driven by savings which originate from growth itself as in Mankiw et al. (1992, p. 410) - this would cause a reverse causality problem and, as a result, endogeneity, which would distort our OLS estimates. Secondly, in contrast to panel data models, a growth regression allows for inclusion of constant variables and their proxies as dummies, which is not possible in the dynamic framework or when using panel data transformation to purge unobserved effects with an exception to the random effects method as in Wooldridge (2002, p. 257). The drawbacks of this method are: the risk of heteroskedasticity and measurement errors. Heteroscedasticity can be tested and resolved with robust standard errors[3] as stated in Wooldridge (2002, p. 162). The measurement error is a different problem: initial values can represent only a random snapshot of the given variables of interest, or the proxy selection may be imprecise. We can deal with the first type of the measurement error by taking the average of the first several years, whereas in the case of the second type, after selecting the most appropriate proxy, one can only rely on the available data and its integrity. In addition, we could identify the outliers and exclude or treat them - this will be performed in our growth regressions. One could also check for changes in data collection or measurement methodology, since during a long period of time measurement of macroeconomic variables might have evolved. For example, if one has to measure the GRP per capita in the 1970s in the Soviet Russia, then a measurement error would most likely occur due to measurement particularities of the planned economy.

1.3.1 Cross-section growth regressions

The first paper with growth regressions applied to the growth empirics was Barro (1991). As Barro (1991, p. 407) mentions, the main story behind the growth regressions is not only to estimate the impact of growth determinants, but also to estimate the convergence effect, caused by the diminishing returns to "reproducible capital". The effect in question is the so-called β-convergence which has certain implications: rich countries would grow slower than poor. Barro (1991, p. 414) uses OLS estimation with robust standard errors to eliminate heteroscedasticity and includes initial values of enrolment rates as a proxy for human capital, averages fertility, mortality, assassination rates and other variables, and uses dummies for regions. Barro

[3] In addition, robust standard errors help to minimize the small sample bias.

(1991, p. 428) himself does not successfully resolve all the issues: he mentions potential endogeneity of average investment to income ratio. Besides the assassination rates variable as in Barro (1991, p. 432) may not the best proxy for property rights. A more sophisticated approach to explain the impact of property rights on economic performance was implemented by Acemoglu et al. (2001), who used settler mortality[4] as a causal instrument for endogenous expropriation risks which have a negative impact on economic performance[5]. Nevertheless, one has to admit that the key findings of the early growth regressions as stated in Sala-i-Martin (1994, p. 741) were: "education was an important determinant of the growth rate", "investment was positively correlated with growth" (however, without a causal relationship), "the coefficient of the initial level of income was significantly negative". Sala-i-Martin (1994, pp. 743-744) specifies that according to the neoclassical prediction the growth rate of an economy would be inversely related to the distance from its steady state and the convergence rate of "roughly 2 percent per year" out of Barro's growth regressions corresponds with this statement. One has to note that the convergence coefficients differ from one specification to another and also depend on the sample and the time dimension. For example, once the time frames include years of economic depressions in the analysis, then the growth rates would be slower and thus the convergence coefficient, perhaps, lower - this will be further discussed with the help of empirical estimations.

The first growth regressions were applied to countries at a macroeconomic level; however, the same tool can be applied to regions. As it was shown in Kufenko (2012, p. 5), Russia enjoys impressive regional economic heterogeneity, which allows us to exploit this feature and apply empirical tools to the Russian regions. One of the first systemic attempts to do so was Drobyshevsky et al. (2005). As stated in Drobyshevsky et al. (2005, p. 54-59), the speed of unconditional β-convergence for the Russian regions during 1994-2002 was approximately 0.825% per year or 6.6% divided by 8 years. As stated in Dobler and Hagemann (2011, p. 26), at the beginning of the 1990s Russia experienced the so-called "big bang" or a rapid and radical transformation from the planned economy to a market one and the longer the period of consideration is - the better.

Even though some researchers suggest that Russia has never become a truly market economy as in Hedlund (2008), still the liberalization and privatization did open the door for higher economic growth rates. One should note that privatization partially solved some old problems, such as the ab-

---

4 One has to note that the settler mortality data contained certain flaws according to Albouy (2008) and thus the results obtained are subject to further debates.

5 It is important to distinguish growth regressions from performance regressions, where the dependent variable is indicated in levels, rather than growth rates.

sence of private property and entrepreneurship, but also created the new ones, such as concentrated ownership and oligarchic structures: as in Guriev and Rachinsky (2005, pp. 135-136), oligarchs in Russia possess enormous market power and in 2003 around 42.4% of employment could be attributed to the firms owned by different oligarchs. Guriev and Rachinsky (2005, p. 144) show a positive relation between productivity growth and oligarchic ownership; however, they doubt the efficiency of oligarchs at a micro level compared to other types of owners, such as foreign, federal or regional ones.

Nevertheless, in Russia we would expect a higher convergence effect. Referring to Solanko (2003, pp. 11-12), the unconditional β-convergence coefficient for Russian regional growth during the period 1992-2001 is -0.0299, which represents a 3% convergence based on the 1992 GRP per capita value as the initial point. One of the merits of the above-mentioned paper is the acknowledgement of the existence of the so-called "convergence clubs" among Russian regions as in Solanko (2003, p. 21). In our regressions we will control for that using dummies for the largest cities - this way is preferable to dividing the sample into sub-samples, which would limit the number of observations significantly. Indeed, splitting the data set of 80 regions into 3-4 groups would increase the small sample bias; whereas accounting for regions with largest cities would not change the sample and would help us to additionally control for regions with large urban areas. An explanation to such a low effect of convergence as in Drobyshevsky et al. (2005) can be relatively simple: the 1998 sovereign default and the related financial crisis are partly included in the analysis since the last time point to be selected was 2001 and this year may still capture some remaining effects of the crisis. As stated in Dobler and Hagemann (2011, pp. 15-17), 1998-1999 were among the toughest years for the Russian economy due to the default and significant rouble devaluation. Obviously, this fact decreased economic growth rates and thus smaller growth rates might be the reason for such small convergence effect. So far, we have mostly mentioned the unconditional convergence; however, obviously after adding other variables the magnitude of the effect would change. The above-mentioned facts allow us to make the following statement:

Proposition 3. *The empirically estimated unconditional and conditional β-convergence effect depends on the model specification; overall and initial time periods selection, and estimation method.*

Indeed, the meta analysis of convergence studies confirms this. Recent studies on Russian regions using different methodologies include Guriev and Vakulenko (2012), which represents an expanded research, also related to the study of Gluschenko (2010). The latter work is a meta analysis of all growth studies on Russian regions. The β-convergence speed of GRP varies: 2% for 1990-1996 in Mikheeva (1999); from 3.48 to 7.86% for 1995-2004 in Melnikov (2005), from 1.57 to 11% for 1999-2004 in Buccellato (2007) as stated in Guriev and Vakulenko (2012, p. 54). The results of the meta analysis suggest that the authors find divergence as well.

1.3.2 Dynamic panel data

Having considered growth regressions, we should also examine more modern techniques such as dynamic panel data estimators. Another view on β-convergence is the time-series property of income: if we are to observe convergence, then the lagged level of income would have a negative impact on the current growth. In other words, the higher the previous income level, the smaller the current growth. As stated in Wooldridge (2002, p. 304), unless valid and relevant instruments for the lagged dependent variable are used, adding such a variable into the panel data model would cause violation of exogeneity. Anderson and Hsiao (1981) were among the first scholars to propose a consistent Maximum Likelihood estimator for an autoregressive model for panel data. Nevertheless, as stated in Anderson and Hsiao (1981, p. 57), such estimator would be consistent for all explanatory variables only if the number of time periods (further T) is fixed and the number of groups (further N) is infinite, in the reverse case some of the coefficients may not be consistent. The main contribution of this paper was a suggestion of using further lags of the dependent variable as instruments of the first lag, included in the model, as in Anderson and Hsiao (1981, p. 59). Arellano and Bond (1991) went further and introduced differenced equations and lagged differences as instruments: as stated in Arellano and Bond (1991, p. 291), the usage of lagged differences as instruments for differenced lags of the dependent variable. The work on the improvements to the above-mentioned estimator continued: Arellano and Bover (1995, p. 48) proposed using "lagged differences of the dependent variable as instruments for the equation in levels" and "lagged levels of the dependent variable as instruments for the equation in first differences". As stated in Blundell and Bond (1998, p. 116), the extended GMM estimator performs much better in terms of efficiency than the "basic first-differenced" GMM estimator. This technique is applied to a system of equations in levels and differences with a two-step estimation. As in the case with the OLS growth regressions, the system GMM approach as in Blundell and Bond (1998) has certain advantages as well as drawbacks: firstly, it is a panel data estimator allowing us to take advantage of the cross-section dimension and time, which is necessary to capture the dynamics of growth and the effect of growth determinants in time; secondly, it allows us to capture the auto-regressive effect and include lagged levels or differences of the dependent variable which is crucial for empirics of the convergence process. In fact, system GMM allows us to have a different perspective on β-convergence, depending on the model specification: if the dependent variable is a growth rate, of, for example, the income, then by including the lagged level of income we would be able to check which effect has an increase of the income level in the previous period on the current growth rate (the β-convergence hypothesis assumes a negative impact); whereas, if the dependent variable is a growth rate or a level of income, by including the appropriate lagged moment, that is lagged growth rate or lagged level respectively, into the specification we check how strong the autoregressive process is and whether the acceleration is positive. Moreover, as noted in Young et al. (2008, pp. 6-7), β-convergence effect would increase the dispersion and variation of income (which can be empirically measured with the help of standard deviation) since poorer countries would be growing faster than rich. This statement will be tested empirically in our work. Thus, it is highly probable that if we discover β-convergence, the σ-convergence would not be present, unless the time span is long enough to capture countries or/and regions arriving at their steady states. This will be considered in the empirical section.

The main drawback of the system GMM is that it requires enormous number of instruments to be included in the estimation, this can be mitigated by collapsing the instrument matrix as in Blundell and Bond (1998, p. 126). Roodman (2006, p. 23) suggests that collapsing is a reasonable option, since in some cases the number of instruments approaches the number of observations - in those cases the estimation package "xtabond2", which was used in this work, issues a special warning. Another solution is to limit the number of lags, since system GMM uses all of the available lags as instruments, setting lag limits would also decrease the number of instruments. So far, econometric literature has not provided a distinct and reasonable answer on which number of instruments is optimal or which proportion of observations to instruments is preferable. The number of instruments itself is an issue; however, another important problem is their weakness, as mentioned in Blundell and Bond (1998, pp. 120-121). Naturally, another problem arises when the instruments are strong - this can hint at serious autocorrelation: thus, for example as in Blundell and Bond (1998, pp. 121-123), the behaviour of the system would depend on the "non-centrality" parameter. In certain cases the system is determined to explode - such situations are similar to the conventional understanding of stationary and non-stationary systems as in Hamilton (1994, pp. 45-46). One of the ways to test the stability in the system GMM framework is to verify if the dependent variable is stationary. An additional test would be the white-noise test on residuals, since we assume that our exogenous shocks are a serially uncorrelated, zero-mean, constant and finite variance process as in Hamilton (1994, pp. 47-48) which is a stronger restriction on residuals compared to the stationarity assumption. As for the validity and relevancy of the instruments used, as in Chao et al. (2014, p. 2), the well-established Sargan and Hansen tests of the validity of the over-identifying restrictions can be sensitive to number of instruments or heteroscedasticity. One should note that the Sargan test assumes homoscedasticity, whereas the Hansen test uses a heteroscedasticity consistent weighting matrix as stated in Chao et al. (2014, p. 8). This is extremely important since Windmeijer (2005) finds that the errors of the two-step efficient system GMM estimator are downward biased, which requires a correction. Since the errors are corrected, the "xtabond2" package issues an appropriate warning making the Sargan test irrelevant. However, the Hansen test would be also sensitive in terms of the number of instruments - the "xtabond2" package reports a warning in case of too many instruments as well. Another issue of the system GMM technique is the autoregressive effect itself: as Achen (2001, p. 6) notes, that a lagged dependent variable may have a "dominating" effect and drain explanatory power away for other exogenous variables included in the model - this threat is highly relevant if there is autocorrelation in the residuals or/and in the dependent variable. We can avoid this problem by testing the residuals, and checking if the autoregressive coefficient is far from unity, which is highly desired. Thus an autoregressive effect can be inflated due to the presence of artifacts in errors. To sum up, the potential caveats of the two-step system GMM are: high number of instruments, especially with high T and small N when the number of instruments approaches the number of observations; sensitivity of Sargan and Hansen validity tests to heteroscedasticity and large number of instruments respectively; requirement of using robust errors and Windmeijer (2005) correction for the efficient two-step estimator; the threat of artifacts in errors and inflated autoregressive coefficient. Nevertheless, once we know the potential dangers, we can minimize the risks and account for certain issues. Knowing these details about the two-step system GMM estimator will help us to implement the related technique to our best knowledge in the empirical section of this chapter.

Let us now consider empirical research where the given estimator was applied. One of the first successful attempts to apply the efficient two-step system GMM to growth empirics was Bond et al. (2001). The authors tested OLS, Within Group estimator (further WG, which is similar to fixed effects as in Wooldridge (2002, p. 268) and involves within transformation to obtain deviations from the within group mean values), GMM with an equation in first differences and system GMM. The main merit of the given work is not only the practical application of the above-mentioned estimators, but the formulation of a certain specification, best suitable for capturing β-convergence in a dynamic dimension: in Bond et al. (2001, pp. 15-16) the authors discuss different model specifications, for example, the growth regression where first difference of income is explained by the lagged level of income and other exogenous variables or a level equation with a lagged income included (the latter specification was also applied in Kufenko (2012, p. 12), or an equation in first differences, where a lagged first difference of income is used as a proxy for β-convergence.Bond et al. (2001, pp. 31-33) arrive at a specification when the growth rate of income is explained by the lagged level of income and growth rates (as well as levels) of other variables. From our point of view, this specification is the most appropriate: it allows us to trace the impact of the levels of income on growth as in the well-established growth regressions. One should note that these specifications are both considered in Islam (1995, pp. 1134-1136) as valid models for estimating convergence. In Kufenko (2012, p. 12) the lagged real GRP per capita level had a strong positive effect on the subsequent levels with a coefficient of 0.717. This could hint at autocorrelation; however, the specification included time controls, the coefficient was relatively distant from unity and the respective Arellano-Bond test statistics was at a sufficient level to accept the hypothesis of no autocorrelation at 5%, and other levels. In Kufenko (2012, p. 12), the actual speed of convergence was 5.5% according to the Islam (1995, pp. 1135) methodology and $t = 6$ periods. We will apply this method of calculating the speed of convergence later and add a technical note. In this chapter we try a different specification from Bond et al. (2001), treat the explanatory variables as endogenous, include time controls, collapse the instrument matrix to outmaneuver the problem of too many instruments and verify that the residuals are white noise.

Another interesting example is the application of system GMM to the Russian regions in Ledyaeva and Linden (2008). In the above-mentioned paper one two-step system GMM estimation results fail to meet the Arellano-Bond autocorrelation test, as stated in Ledyaeva and Linden (2008, p. 94). This test will be performed in our estimation as well. The authors themselves confirm the fact of autocorrelation and the autoregressive coefficient is even above unity in one of the specifications. The dynamic β-convergence effect of 1.24% from other specifications is postulated in Ledyaeva and Linden (2008, p. 95) as one of the main findings. However, one should carefully rely on these results since the authors report only the Sargan test under the two-step estimation, which as in Chao et al. (2014) is not suitable in this situation - the Hansen test would be advisable. Another issue of Ledyaeva and Linden (2008) is that they do not report the number of instruments used. A far better example of system GMM application is a paper on FDI issued by the Deutsche Bank: Pashinova and Strasky (2012); however, even there the authors do not specify instruments. We consider transparency and integrity as priorities in any research, and in the empirical part of this chapter we will issue a full report on the applied two-step system GMM estimation.

Let us now proceed to describing the data set. For the growth regressions and for the dynamic estimation, the composition of regions will slightly change, as well as the variables. Therefore, we need to display the descriptive statistics as well as brief explanations and sources.

1.4 Data

The core of the dataset consists of the data, comprised from the Goskomstat of Russia (Federal State Statistics Service), publication on the Social and Economic indicators of the Russian regions. Real variables are obtained by deflating, in other words, removing CPI price dynamics from the nominal values. Thus growth rates of real values are cleared from inflation.

Table 2. Data for cross-section OLS growth regressions

Variable	Obs	Mean	Std. Dev.	Min	Max	Description
growth9507	79	146.389	40.474	67.749	285.215	real GRP per capita growth rate, 1995-2007
growth9507/T (avg_growth)	79	12.199	3.373	5.646	23.768	annual real GRP per capita growth rate, 1995-2007
ln_realgrpstart_95	79	8.572	0.572	7.281	10.253	log of real GRP per capita level in 1995
ln_real_grppc_00	79	10.057	0.559	8.617	11.944	log of real GRP per capita level in 2000
educ_share_00	79	21.153	4.945	13.100	41.300	percentage of employed population with higher education in 2000
ln_real_invpc_9596	79	8.392	0.561	6.538	10.782	log of average real fixed investments per capita during 1995-1996
buro_ratio_9596	79	1.962	0.568	0.589	3.762	average percentage of civil servants (public officials and bureaucrats) in employed population during 1995-1996
oil_pc_9596	79	1.39362	7.069	0	62.39	average per capita tonns of oil and gas condensate extracted during 1995-1996
democ_9101	79	27.949	6.228	14	45	average basic Carnegie index for democracy, value for 1991-2001
distmoscow	79	2358.963	2730.673	0	11876	distance from Moscow, kilometers
large_city	79	0.063	0.244	0	1	largest cities: Moscow, Saint-Petersburg, Novosibirsk, Sverdlovsk, Nizhniy Novgorod

Data: Goskomstat, Cernegie Center, Moscow, Abramov (1965)

The total number of regions in the dataset is 79. There are 83 regions overall; however, due to various military conflicts in the Chechnya republic most of the data from this region is missing, so the feasible data involves 79[6] regions and the data for the Chechnya republic is excluded from estimations. The other 3 regions are in fact integral parts of the Arkhangesk oblast

[6] These 79 regions are: the Belgorod oblast, the Bryansk oblast, the Vladimir oblast, the Voronezh oblast, the Ivanovo oblast, the Kaluga oblast, the

and the Tyumen oblast and usually are considered within their boundaries. Total list of regions, appearing in this work, can be found in Appendix.

This data will be used for growth regressions as well as for the computations necessary for the convergence verification. Nominal GRP per capita values in rubles were deflated using the regional CPI inflation in order to receive real GRP per capita. The same was applied to fixed investments per capita. Real GRP per capita levels in 1995 and 2000 were taken as a proxy for the starting reference point and an intermediate reference point. The share of employed population with a university (or higher) degree is taken as a proxy for human capital as in Koritzky (2010). The earliest measurement is available for 2000. Real fixed investments per capita represent physical capital and the share of civil servants in employed population represents a ratio and accounts for both: bureaucrats as in Libman (2012b) and labour. One should highlight the fact that Libman (2012b, p. 1333) constructs a ratio of civil servants to regional population, therefore treating the bureaucrats as a part of population. We use the ratio of civil servants in employed population, therefore treating the bureaucrats as a part of employed population. Obviously, one could also obtain number of bureaucrats per capita. For the latter variables we take averages between 1995 and 1996 - this technique was applied to certain variables in Barro (1991) since averages are more representative than a snapshot from one particular year. Average oil and gas extraction per capita during 1995 and 1996 represents a proxy for

---

Kostroma oblast, the Kursk oblast, the Lipetsk oblast, the Moskovskaya oblast, the Orlovskaya oblast, the Ryazan oblast, the Smolensk oblast, the Tambov oblast, the Tver oblast, the Tula oblast, the Yaroslavl oblast, Moscow city, the Karelia republic, the Komi republic, the Arkhangelsk oblast, the Vologda oblast, the Kaliningrad oblast, the Leningrad oblast, the Murmansk oblast, the Novgorod oblast, the Pskov oblast, Saint-Petersburg city, the Adygeya republic, the Dagestan republic, the Ingushetia republic, the Kabardino-Balkaria republic, the Kalmykia republic, the Karachay-Cherkessia republic, the Northern Osetia-Alania republic, the Krasnodar krai, the Stavropol krai, the Astrakhan oblast, the Volgograd oblast, the Rostov oblast, the Bashkortostan republic, the Mari El republic, the Mordovia republic, the Tatarstan republic, the Udmurt republic, the Chuvashia republic, the Perm krai, the Kirov oblast, the Nizhegorodskaya oblast, the Orenburg oblast, the Penza oblast, the Samara oblast, the Saratov oblast, the Ulyanovsk oblast, the Kurgan oblast, the Sverdlovsk oblast, the Tyumen oblast, the Chelyabinsk oblast, the Altay republic, the Buryat republic, the Tuva republic, the Khakassia republic, the Altai krai, the Krasnoyarsk krai, the Irkutsk oblast, the Kemerovo oblast, the Novosibirsk oblast, the Omsk oblast, the Tomsk oblast, the Chitinskaya oblast, the Yakutia (Sakha) republic, the Kamchatka krai, the Primorye krai, the Khabarovsk krai, the Amur oblast, the Magadan oblast, the Sakhalin oblast, the Jewish autonomous oblast, the Chukotka okrug - sorted in an original order as in Goskomstat.

the development of extraction and the carbon resource abundance. Potentially one could find different proxies for the resource abundance; however, as we see in the next chapter, which focuses on the resource curse, this is one of the most appropriate proxies for Russia, bearing in mind the availability of the data. The democracy index average value for 1991 to 2001 was taken from the Carnegie Center dataset prepared by Petrov and Titkov[7]. The latter variable is a proxy for democracy: since Libman (2012a) suggests that there is a non-linear relation between growth and democracy, a non-parametric estimator would be more appropriate as in Tsybakov (2009, p. 31-34). Nevertheless, we control for democracy in our growth regressions. The distance from Moscow was taken from Abramov (1965) - this variable represents a proxy for spatial centralization. In addition, we account for regions with the largest cities: Moscow, Saint-Petersburg, Novosibirsk, Sverdlovsk and Nizhniy Novgorod. The real GRP per capital growth rate between 1995 and 2007 is the overall growth rate, which can be annualized by dividing the values by the number of years. Thus we can annualize the growth rate as in Gluschenko (2010, p. 11) or the effect - the end result will be the same. It is noteworthy that we could not include some variables, for example, proxies for technology, due to the fact that their measurement started in 2000 and this could potentially cause additional endogeneity issues or multicollinearity with other variables dated by 2000.

The dataset for the dynamic model is smaller. Since we had to include technology in our analysis, we had to limit our dataset to 57 regions[8] since for other regions the related data was missing. Therefore, we make a separate table for the data on the 57 regions for the dynamic estimation for

[7] Further details on the data: http://atlas.socpol.ru/indexes/

[8] These 57 regions are: the Belgorod oblast, the Bryansk oblast, the Vladimir oblast, the Voronezh oblast, the Kaluga oblast, the Kostroma oblast, the Kursk oblast, the Moskovskaya oblast, the Orlovskaya oblast, the Smolensk oblast, the Tver oblast, the Tula oblast, the Yaroslavl oblast, Moscow city, the Karelia republic, the Komi republic, the Arkhangelsk oblast, the Kaliningrad oblast, the Leningrad oblast, the Murmansk oblast, the Novgorod oblast, Saint-Petersburg city, the Dagestan republic, the Kabardino-Balkaria republic, the Krasnodar krai, the Astrakhan oblast, the Volgograd oblast, the Rostov oblast, the Bashkortostan republic, the Mari El republic, the Mordovia republic, the Tatarstan republic, the Udmurt republic, the Chuvashia republic, the Perm krai, the Nizhegorodskaya oblast, the Orenburg oblast, the Penza oblast, the Samara oblast, the Saratov oblast, the Ulyanovsk oblast, the Kurgan oblast, the Sverdlovsk oblast, the Tyumen oblast, the Chelyabinsk oblast, the Buryat republic, the Krasnoyarsk krai, the Irkutsk oblast, the Kemerovo oblast, the Novosibirsk oblast, the Omsk oblast, the Tomsk oblast, the Chitinskaya oblast, the Yakutia (Sakha) republic, the Khabarovsk krai, the Magadan oblast, the Sakhalin oblast - sorted in an original order as in Goskomstat.

2000-2007. The technology proxy is the number of created new technologies per capita in the given regions. This is the most suitable proxy out of the data on patents. Other patent types include inventions and prototype models for which the data is also limited. The time controls are necessary to avoid autocorrelation as in Blundell and Bond (1998). The data in Table 3 is indicated in growth rates.

Table 3. Data for FD and two-step System GMM

Variable	Obs	Mean	Std. Dev.	Min	Max	Description
$\Delta y_{i,t}$	328	0.235	0.080	-0.001	0.558	growth rate of real GRP per capita
$\ln y_{i,t-1}$	328	10.891	0.688	9.216	13.442	lagged level of logarithm of real GRP per capita
$\Delta realinv\ pc_{i,t}$	328	0.337	0.281	-0.489	1.237	growth rate of real fixed investments per capita
$\Delta labour\ share_{i,t}$	328	0.0108	0.0122	-0.0259	0.0831	growth rate of share of employed population
$\Delta tech\ pc_{i,t}$	328	0.0219	0.6601	-1.9362	2.8454	growth rate of patented new technologies per capita
third	328	0.399	0.491	0	1	3 year period: 2001, 2002, 2003
fourth	328	0.445	0.498	0	1	3 year period: 2004, 2005, 2006
fifth	328	0.155	0.363	0	1	1 year period: 2007

Data: Goskomstat

1.5 Empirical strategy and results

Let us now proceed to the empirical estimation. One of the primary tasks of the empirical part of this chapter is to verify σ-convergence and β-convergence (unconditional and conditional). The second row of tasks is to investigate growth determinants with the help of growth regressions as in Barro (1991) or as in Gluschenko (2010), and dynamic two-step system GMM estimation as in Ledyaeva and Linden (2008).

We will start with the simplest task and plot the development of cross-section standard deviations of the logarithm of the real GRP per capita. We have previously mentioned that in case of σ-convergence, we would expect the variability of real GRP per capita to decrease with time as in Young et al. (2008, p. 3). In this case we consider all available regions and calculate standard deviation for each year for all the regions. In order to capture the 2008 crisis we have appended the years up to 2010; however, only for the real GRP per capita.

It is necessary to mark two time points: the default crisis of 1998 and the arrival of the global financial crisis to Russia in the late 2008. This explains the time-specific variation of the cross-section variation: on Figure

Fig. 3. σ-convergence

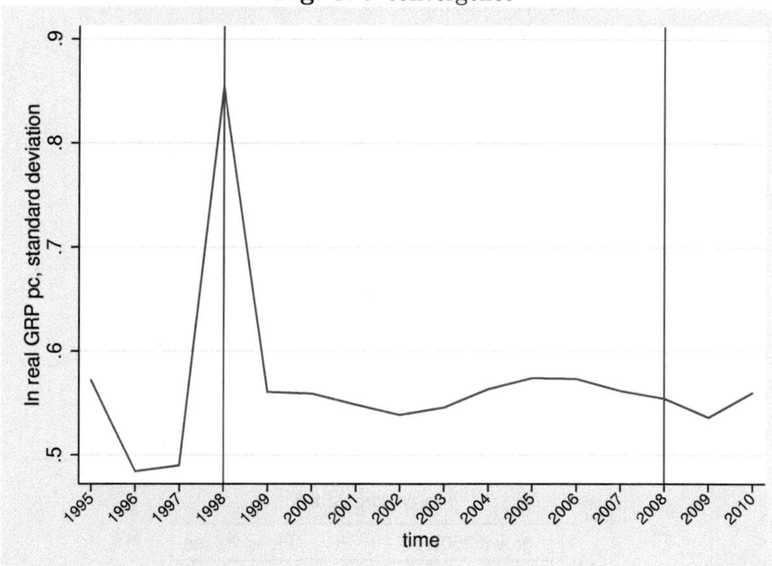

Data: Goskomstat

3 we see a sharp jump in standard deviation in 1998 which would mean a non-uniform influence of the 1998 crisis on the GRP, or in other words, some regions were affected more than others, causing sharp contrasts; however, in 2008 we observe a decrease in standard deviation, suggesting that the impact of the 2008 financial turmoil was relatively uniform for the regions. This is also confirmed by the panel graphs in the Appendix. Nevertheless, we see a small increase in standard deviation in 2010. Thus we formulate the following statement:

Proposition 4. *Empirical findings suggest absence of σ-convergence in real GRP per capita in 79 Russian regions during 1995-2010.*

Consequently, we proceed to the unconditional β-convergence. Figure 4 represents a scatter plot with the average annual growth between 1995 and 2007 on the y-axis and the reference value of logarithm of the real GRP per capita in 1995 on the x-axis: a negative relation is obvious; however, one has to estimate the slope of the trend line and check the robustness of this effect. This finding suggests a certain evidence of the unconditional β-convergence.

We find it necessary to investigate whether regions are converging to the real GRP per capita level of Moscow, one of the richest regions. Figure 5 has an additional useful tool displayed: the 45 degree line which marks constant

Fig. 4. Unconditional β-convergence

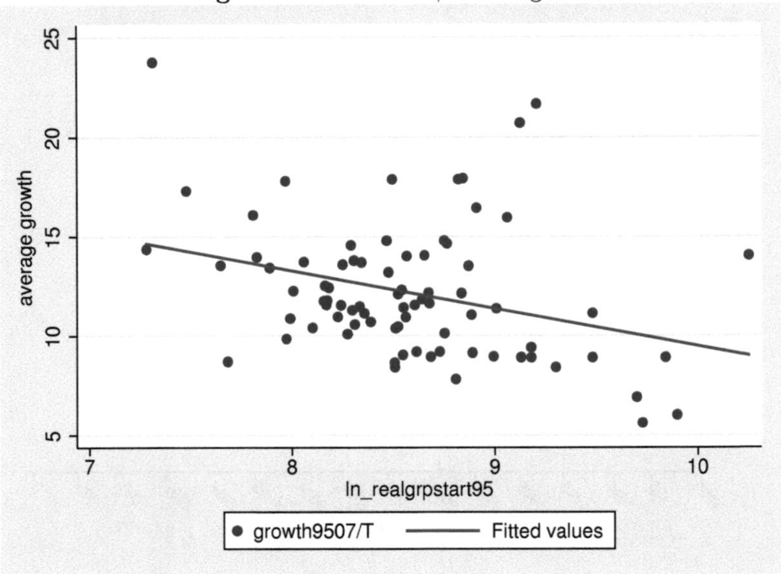

Data: Goskomstat

growth in relation to Moscow's GRP. If the region finds itself exactly on the line, this would mean that the share of the given region's GRP per capita did not significantly change from 1995 to 2010. On the contrary, if the region is below the benchmark line, it would be worse off, compared to Moscow.

The most successful regions find themselves above the benchmark line. The evidence of convergence to Moscow is vague: most of the regions are on or marginally above the reference line compared to Moscow, which hints at the absence of catching up to the level of Moscow. The majority of regions lie below 1 on the x-axis, which indicates that their real GRP per capita was lower than the value for Moscow in 1995, and the ratio to GRP of Moscow is stable. Most astonishing is that a large part of these regions lies below 0.5 on the y-axis which means that in 2010 (as well as in 1995) their real GRP per capita was less than 50% of the value for Moscow. This allows us to assume that the output of the majority of regions is not catching up, as in Abramovitz (1986, pp. 386-387) and rather follows the output of Moscow. Most of the regions lie below 50% of real GRP per capita of Moscow city, which is a sharp contrast. Thus, we would like to highlight the presence of GRP per capita disparities and sharp contrasts between regions. Here we have to formulate an important proposition, supported by the empirical findings:

Fig. 5. Catching up to Moscow

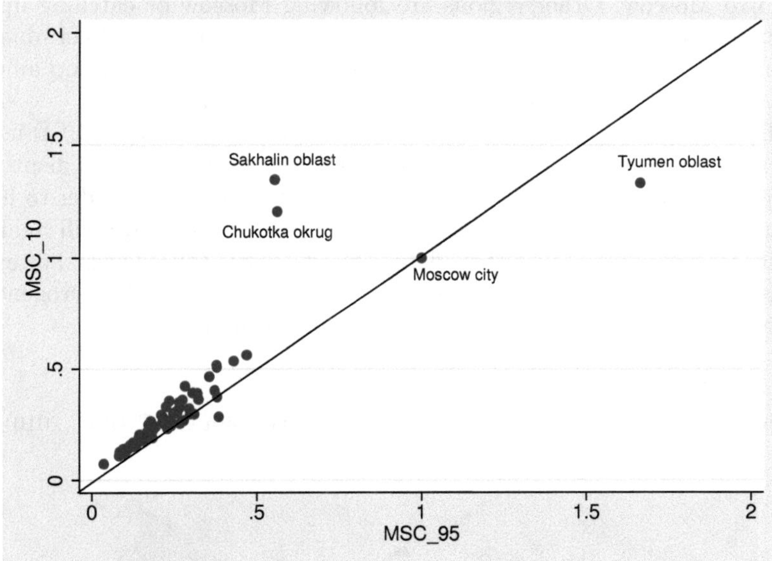

Data: Goskomstat

Proposition 5. *Having found evidence of unconditional β-convergence among 79 regions during 1995-2010, we have established substantial regional disparities and absence of catching up to the real GRP per capita level of Moscow among most of the regions.*

Indeed, in 2010 the top-5 richest Russian regions were: the Sakhalin oblast, the Tyumen oblast, the Chukotka okrug, Moscow city and the Komi republic. The first three regions, as well as the fifth one, enjoy a low population density and a high output due to resource endowments (oil and gas in the Tyumen oblast and the Komi republic and gold and minerals in the Chukotka okrug and the Sakhalin oblast). Moscow as the capital enjoys administrative resources and human capital rather than natural endowments.

However, not all of them are "leaders" as in Abramovitz (1986, p. 396): the Sakhalin oblast and the Chukotka okrug lie above the reference line (the Sakhalin oblast takes advantage of the trade links with China and Japan whereas Chukotka enjoys large amount of diverse natural resources); however, the Tyumen oblast clearly lags behind Moscow. Another region which is significantly lagging behind is the Vologda oblast: in 1995 the ratio of real GRP per capita of Vologda oblast to Moscow city was 0.38 whereas in 2010 it was 0.286. The Omsk, the Tomsk, the Samara oblast, the Karelia republic is also lagging behind Moscow. On the contrary, the Primorye krai, the Komi republic and Saint-Petersburg have shown modest signs of catching up to Moscow. Other regions are following Moscow or catching up at marginally small rates. Further we will investigate empirical determinants of growth among Russian regions; however, analysis of catching up among Russian regions is an interesting topic for further research.

The 2010 spatial distribution of real GRP per capita in PPP USD using the conversion factor suggested in the OECD database (15.6)[9] is displayed on Figure 6. We have appended the year 2010 to our data in order to have the most recent available snapshot of the regions. Further we will analyse growth determinants rather than determinants of the GRP levels; however, at this step of our research, it is essential to consider regional heterogeneity in Russia which offers fruitful grounds for empirical analysis.

Fig. 6. Regional heterogeneity in real GRP per capita (PPP USD, 2010)

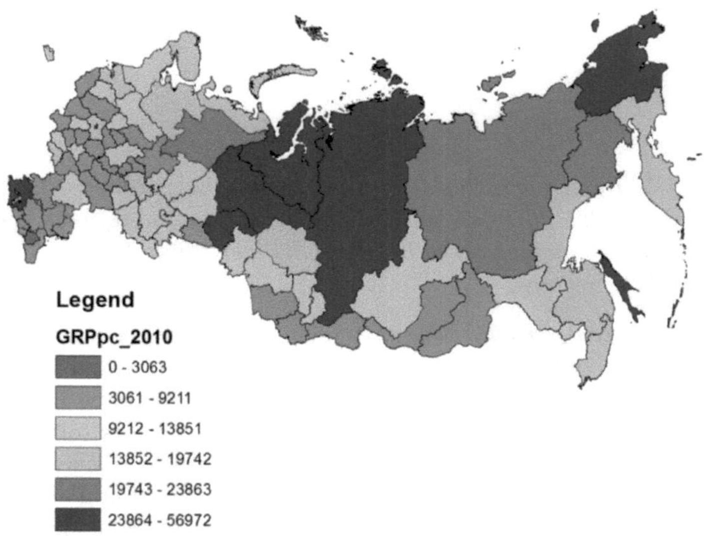

Data: Goskomstat

We can proceed and formulate the empirical strategy for our regional growth regressions. By formulating one model with a proxy for β-convergence, a vector of initial or intermediate values of growth determinants and a vector of controls, we introduce flexibility and perform estimation of several specifications adding variables to ensure robustness of our results. This ap-

[9] Taken from http://stats.oecd.org/

proach resembles the simplified version of the so-called "extreme bounds" methodology from the "Levine and Renelt" critique mentioned in Sala-i-Martin (1994, p. 742). The essence of this approach is simply testing the robustness of the variables of interest by increasing the number of controls up to an extreme bound when the significance of the given variables vanishes. In such case, the variable would be fragile and otherwise, robust. As in Sala-i-Martin (1994, p. 742), most of the growth determinants are fragile, and only investments and initial income is robust at the cross-country level. In our opinion, obtaining elasticity coefficients for growth determinants is sufficient; however, testing the robustness is far more important.

Another issue of cross-section growth regressions is identifying and treating the outliers, or extremely influential observations with high residuals and high predicted values, known as leverage. As in Libman (2012b, pp. 1338-1339), "the typical problem of analysis of federations is that the data contain outliers". These occasionally have a large fraction of the explanatory power. For identifying the outliers we will plot leverage and normalized residuals squared using a special command "lvr2plot". We will treat the outliers in two ways: excluding and comparing our results with included outliers and applying a robust regression based on the Cook's distance as in Li (1985, p. 282-293). It is noteworthy that this method is capable of identifying single outliers and performs worse if we have clusters of outliers as in Verardi and Croux (2009, p. 442). Due to that reason we test on heteroscedasticity. Unfortunately the estimators suggested in Verardi and Croux (2009, p. 444) lack measures of fit and the Stata script "mmregress" does not allow to obtain data necessary for computation of R-squared, so we have to use the standard "rreg" command and "rregfit" for the measures of fit to implement a regression robust to outliers assuming homoscedasticity which was confirmed in previous tests. At this step we need to sum up the challenges for the growth regressions applied to the Russian regional data:

Proposition 6. *When formulating the empirical strategy for regional growth regressions, one should specifically address the issues of: endogeneity and causality, heteroscedasticity, measurement errors, multicollinearity, omitted variables and outliers.*

Not all of these issues cause the OLS estimates to be biased; however, we have to exercise due diligence to discuss and check all of the above-mentioned issues to produce plausible results.

1.5.1 Estimation results: cross-section growth regressions

Let us formulate the following empirical model:

$$\ln\left(y_{i,T}/y_{i,t=0}\right)/T = \beta_0+\beta_1 y_{i,t=0}+\beta_2\bar{x}_{i,t0,t1}+\beta_3 x_{i,T-t}+\beta_4 z_{i,T-t}+u_{i,t} \quad (12)$$

where $\ln(y_{i,T}/y_{i,t=0})/T$ is the average annual growth rate during the period 1995-2007; $y_{i,t=0}$ is the level of initial income in the starting point; $\bar{x}_{i,t0,t1}$ is a vector of variables, averaged between 1995 and 1996 years; $x_{i,T-t}$ is a vector of variables for other years during $T-t$, e. g. 2000; $z_{i,T-t}$ is a vector of controls including constant variables; β is a coefficient; $u_{i,t}$ is an error term. When applicable, the logarithms of the variables were used.

Empirical model based on equation (12) has several specifications. Thus, there are 3 specifications for growth regressions: (12.1) represents unconditional β-convergence; (12.2) includes share of employed population with higher education in 2000, real fixed investments per capita, average during 1995-1996 and the share of bureaucrats in the employed population during 1995-1996 as growth determinants in a conditional β-convergence model; specifications (12.2), (12.3), (12.4) differ by the treatment of outliers: in (12.2) the outliers are included; in (12.3) we exclude the outliers; in (12.4) we perform a robust regression with Huber weights, bi-weighting and the default tuning parameter of 7. In specification (12.2) the 8 outliers are: the Ivanovo oblast, Moscow city, the Dagestan republic, the Karachay-Cherkessia republic, Northern Osetia-Alania republic, the Astrakhan oblast, the Saratov oblast, the Yakutia (Sakha) republic. Specification (12.5) additionally controls for 2000 year income level, resource abundance (oil and gas condensate per capita extraction 1995-1996), distance from Moscow and regions with 5 largest cities. In specification (12.5) the 7 outliers are: the Moskovskaya oblast, the Dagestan republic, the Kirov oblast, the Yakutia (Sakha) republic, the Primorye krai, the Sakhalin oblast, the Tyumen oblast. Specification (12.6) excludes the outliers, whereas specification (12.7) treats them as in specification (12.4).

We will apply OLS estimation with standard errors and use the Breusch-Pagan/Cook-Weisberg test for heteroskedasticity as in Wooldridge (2002, pp. 126-128). Then we will check for multicollinearity as in Kutner et al. (2004, Chapters 7 and 10) with the Variance Inflation Factor (VIF) and perform an omitted variables specification test as in Ramsey (1969, p. 361) based on an idea of an optimal residual vector. The latter test is crucial since it helps to reveal specification errors in terms of variable selection and as it turns out, in terms of sampling, since the test results can be also influenced by the change of the sample and inclusion or exclusion of the outliers. Due to this reason, we require this test since it can give us a hint at whether the exclusion of the outliers damages the specification quality or not. Cross-verification with the help of these three tests helps us to identify dangers and ensure the quality of our results for which we set the highest priority.

One has to make several additional notes about the tests. The VIF is one of the simplest measures of multicollinearity. As in Obrien (2007, p.

674) a wide range of benchmarks can be used for this indicator from 4 to 10, with a value above the benchmark indicating presence of severe multicollinearity. The VIF factor is derived from stepwise linear regressions of all explanatory variables on each other: each variable receives its own VIF value based on coefficient of determination (R-squared) and the average value is calculated. One should note that this technique gives only approximate information on multicollinearity and Belsley (1987, p. 88) names it a "second best" technique putting more sophisticated indexes on the first place. For the purpose of detecting multicollinearity in our growth regression this method would be sufficient, since none of the specifications reaches even the lowest VIF benchmark of 4. VIF is computed as a due diligence procedure because we assume some correlation between initial GRP per capita value and 1995-1996 average real investments per capita. Due to this reason we do not include squared variables to check for non-linear effects as in Libman (2012a); however, once could potentially sacrifice the absence of multicollinearity for inclusion of non-linear effects.

Another important test is the "regression specification error test" (the Omitted Variable or the OV test) as in Ramsey (1969, p. 361) based on the residuals. The null hypothesis of this test is that the model has no specification errors (or no Omitted Variable Bias) as in Ramsey (1969, pp. 361-362). Otherwise, the independent variables included in the specification have low explanatory power and potentially important variables were omitted. As we have mentioned, we will consider the OV test results with and without outliers to check if the exclusion poses a threat to the specification quality.

Let us discuss the results. The unconditional β-convergence effect from specification (12.1) is 1.895% or around 1.9%. The effect is significant at all levels. This result corresponds to the estimates of other previously mentioned authors. The fit of this specification is low and it fails the OV test at 5% level, which means that growth determinants were omitted. This is a logical conclusion from an unconditional convergence specification.

In specification (12.2), the β-convergence jumps to 2.85% perhaps due to certain collinearity with the explanatory variables; however, the overall VIF is relatively low around 1.34 and none of the variable-specific VIF values exceeds 10. Similar issue has been found in Solanko (2003, p. 18), where the coefficient on the GRP per capita level of 1995 increased after adding variables. As can be concluded from the tables in Barro (1991, pp. 410-413), the β-convergence coefficient may not necessarily decrease in magnitude or significance after adding further variables or controls. The effect of 1% positive change in percentage of employed population with a university degree or higher in 2000 is 0.151% of growth, which is significant at 5% level. Elasticity of real fixed investments per capita has a positive effect of 1.534% on growth which is significant at 10% level. Share of civil servants in employed

Table 4. Basic OLS growth regressions

	OLS			
		all regions	no outliers	robust regression
	(12.1)	(12.2)	(12.3)	(12.4)
VARIABLES	growth	growth	growth	growth
ln_realgdpstart95	-1.895***	-2.855***	-2.036***	-2.728***
	(0.636)	(0.735)	(0.730)	(0.689)
	-2.979	-3.887	-2.789	-3.958
educ_share00		0.151**	0.102	0.136**
		(0.0710)	(0.0814)	(0.0666)
		2.127	1.259	2.046
ln_real_invpc_9596		1.534*	1.035	1.163
		(0.783)	(0.774)	(0.735)
		1.959	1.338	1.584
buro_ratio_9596		-0.723	-0.598	-1.057*
		(0.651)	(0.635)	(0.611)
		-1.111	-0.941	-1.731
Constant	28.44***	22.02***	19.82***	24.70***
	(5.464)	(6.777)	(6.999)	(6.357)
	5.206	3.250	2.832	3.885
Observations	79	79	71	79
R-squared	0.103	0.234	0.135	0.195
Outliers	-	Included	Excluded	Weighted
Adjusted R-squared	0.0917	0.1921	0.0824	0.1514
Homoskedasticity	0.1778	0.6849	0.1247	-
Multicollinearity (mean VIF)	1	1.34	1.34	-
Ramsey OVB test (ovtest; Ho: no OVB)	0.0232	0.1596	0.5041	-

Standard errors in parentheses
*** p<0.01, ** p<0.05, * p<0.1
Weighted: Huber weights and bi-weighting

Source: proprietary estimation

population was not significant; however, this variable had a negative coefficient. Specification (12.2) passes the OV test. These results are valid for the sample with outliers.

As we have mentioned, there are 8 outliers in specification (12.2). This can be seen from the graphs in the Appendix. After removing the Ivanovo oblast, Moscow city, the Dagestan republic, the Karachay-Cherkessia republic, the Northern Osetia-Alania republic, the Astrakhan oblast, the Saratov oblast, the Yakutia (Sakha) republic from the sample, we obtain estimates for specification (12.3). In (12.3) the β-convergence is 2%; however, all other variables lose their significance and the adjusted R-squared is relatively low. Even though the OV test yields plausible results on specification, we proceed to a robust regression and weight the outliers with Huber weights and bi-weighting.

Specification (12.4) applies a robust regression as described in Li (1985, pp. 282-290). Therefore we have no need to manually exclude observations with extreme leverage and large residuals. None of the observations was removed and none received a 0 weight; other regions received weights less than 1 and larger than 0. As we have mentioned before, this is not the only technique available "rreg" package detects only extreme outliers, not the clusters of outliers, as in Verardi and Croux (2009, p. 442); however, for the purposes of this research it is sufficient. In addition, we do not find heteroscedasticity according to the test results, so the robust regression may yield plausible results. The treatment of the outliers allows us to obtain the β-convergence of 2.73%. In specification (12.4) the effect of 1% positive change in percentage of employed population with a university degree or higher in 2000 is 0.136% of growth and the effect of 1% increase in the share of bureaucrats in employed population is -1.057% of growth, which is significant at 10% level. The effect of real fixed investments is 1.16%. It is noteworthy that these results are valid for the treated outliers.

Specification (12.5) introduces 2000 year income level, average oil and gas extraction per capita in 1995-1996, Carnegie Center democracy index for 1991-2001, distance from Moscow in kilometres and a dummy variable for regions with 5 largest cities. Exclusion of the 7 outliers (the Moskovskaya oblast, the Dagestan republic, the Kirov oblast, the Yakutia (Sakha) republic, the Primorye krai, the Sakhalin oblast, the Tyumen oblast as in Appendix) increased the adjusted R-squared as can be seen in specification (12.6), where the adjusted R-squared is 0.3753. Therefore, in this case removing outliers improved the explanatory power of the model and the (12.6) results can be considered as plausible since they pass the OV test and there is no heteroskedasticity in residuals. In specification (12.6) β-convergence is 3.6% and we see a significant positive impact of the real GRP per capital level in 2000. Democracy index, distance from Moscow and large city dummy are also significant.

Last specification (12.7) has the β-convergence of 2.976%, a significant impact of human capital of 0.12%, a significant negative impact of democracy index as found in Libman (2012b, p. 1335), and a significant negative impact of distance from Moscow with 1 additional kilometer distance resulting in a decrease of growth by 0.000370%. Or, in other words, each additional 1000 kilometers distance from Moscow results in a decrease of growth by 0.370%. We have to note that the robust regression "rreg" also has automatically removed one outlier and assigned weight of 0 to two ob-

Table 5. Extended OLS growth regressions

	OLS		
	all regions	no outliers	robust regression
	(12.5)	(12.6)	(12.7)
VARIABLES	growth	growth	growth
ln_realgdpstart95	-3.898***	-3.602***	-2.976***
	(1.259)	(1.025)	(1.024)
	-3.096	-3.513	-2.908
ln_real_grppc_00	2.026	2.590**	1.803
	(1.477)	(1.203)	(1.212)
	1.371	2.153	1.487
educ_share00	0.137*	0.0692	0.120*
	(0.0766)	(0.0588)	(0.0628)
	1.794	1.177	1.905
ln_real_invpc_9596	0.614	-0.0203	0.0260
	(0.949)	(0.771)	(0.773)
	0.647	-0.0263	0.0336
buro_ratio_9596	-0.318	-0.252	-0.214
	(0.849)	(0.670)	(0.693)
	-0.374	-0.377	-0.309
oil_pc9596	0.0684	0.275	0.340
	(0.0594)	(0.190)	(0.204)
	1.151	1.442	1.665
democ_9101	-0.0649	-0.124**	-0.110*
	(0.0713)	(0.0549)	(0.0581)
	-0.910	-2.268	-1.899
distmoscow	-0.000153	-0.000318**	-0.000370***
	(0.000167)	(0.000143)	(0.000136)
	-0.918	-2.223	-2.729
large_city	1.103	2.406*	2.226
	(1.722)	(1.290)	(1.409)
	0.640	1.864	1.580
Constant	19.81**	19.85**	20.40**
	(9.630)	(7.907)	(7.911)
	2.057	2.510	2.579
Observations	79	72	78
R-squared	0.291	0.4545	0.3275
Outliers	Included	Excluded	Weighted
Adjusted R-squared	0.1986	0.3753	0.2385
Homoskedasticity	0.8021	0.2398	-
Multicollinearity (mean VIF)	2.50	2.32	-
Ramsey OVB test (ovtest; Ho: no OVB)	0.5735	0.2451	-

Standard errors in parentheses

*** p<0.01, ** p<0.05, * p<0.1

Weighted: Huber weights and bi-weighting

Source: proprietary estimation

servations due to the fact that for these observations, the Cook's distance, or the measure of leverage and residual size, was larger than one - this is an automated procedure. The automatically removed observation was the Tyumen oblast, whereas the 0 weight was assigned to the Sakhalin oblast and the Dagestan republic. We have listed them as outliers as well earlier in (12.6).

We have to make several notes on the explanatory power of the models in consideration. Some of the researchers enjoy a different set of variables: e.g., Berkowitz and DeJong (2003, p. 345) report R-squared of 0.502 (in the table on the same page the value is 0.491) for policy-driven growth in Russian regions without reporting the adjusted R-squared. A wide range of controls in addition to instumental variables was used in Libman (2012b, p. 1334), where the author reports R-squared of 0.466 to 0.526 for the growth regressions. Libman (2012b, pp. 1335-1338) uses certain variables in absolute values, e.g., oil and gas extraction. Libman (2012b, p. 1333) averages most dependent and independent variables for the period in consideration 2000-2004 and applies intruments. In our research we prefer to use initial values, average first two years or intermediate ones to ensure exogeneity and avoid necessity to apply instrumental variables. In addition, we use per capita transformation since absolute values may capture other size or region-specific effects. Libman (2012b) uses various controls and adds average temperature, which improves the fit. We have to note that even though the fit of our models may appear modest, we report the adjusted R-squared in order to achieve transparency and expose as many details and issues related to the estimation as possible. In our specifications the highest R-squared was 0.4545 and adjusted R-squared was 0.3753; however, one should note that the explanatory power alone does not signal about the good quality of the model: one should not assume an arbitrary heteroscedasticity and rather test for it, and check for multicollinearity and specification errors.

Before drawing a conclusion we should make a note on the diversity of results on convergence and magnitude of coefficients of other variables. The variety of convergence estimates for Russian regions in the literature can be explained not only by the different approach (cross-section or dynamic), specification and time frames, but also the method of obtaining real values. We have used the CPI inflation of the same time period to obtain real GRP per capita values; however, hypothetically, one could apply different deflators and thus obtain different convergence speeds. Therefore, an increase in deflated real GRP leads to increase in growth rates and potentially can lead to an increase in β-convergence. Thus, the convergence estimate is sensitive also to the deflator. Now let us focus on the statements considering β-convergence in our specifications. Let us sum up our empirical findings:

Proposition 7. *According to our findings, the unconditional β-convergence for the Russian regions during 1995-2007 was 1.895% per year (as in specification (12.1); whereas the conditional convergence for the given period was in range from 2.036 to 3.898% as in specifications (12.3) and (12.5). We suggest 2.96%, the average value, as a plausible estimate of the conditional convergence in the given period in the cross-section dimension.*

Further we will show that the convergence effect in the dynamic dimension is slightly different. Regarding fragility and robustness of our variables we should note the following:

Proposition 8. *Real fixed investments per capita and share of bureaucrats in the employed population turned out to be fragile variables, whereas β-convergence was robust in all specifications and share of employed population with higher education, as a proxy for human capital, was robust in some specifications, for example, in (12.2), (12.4), (12.5) and (12.7).*

Last statement summarizes the effects of controls under consideration:

Proposition 9. *The Carnegie democracy index for 1991-2001 is significant in (12.6) and (12.7) and has negative impact; distance from Moscow is significant in (12.6) and (12.7) and has a negative impact represented by a decrease in growth by 0.370 for each additional 1 000 kilometers from Moscow, whereas proxy for regions with 5 largest cities was significant only in (12.6), without the outliers.*

The latter is important, since Libman (2012b, p. 1347) finds a non-linear impact of the Carnegie index for 2000-2004. However, as we have seen from other specifications, this effect is fragile. The difference in our findings can be explained by different time settings for the variables, usage of polynomials and by averaging of the variables for the whole period by other authors.

1.5.2 Estimation results: dynamic panel data

Now let us proceed to the dynamic model and the system GMM estimation. The system GMM allows us to capture convergence in a dynamic setting. Thus we formulate the following model as in Bond et al. (2001, pp. 15-16) to which the "xtabond2" command will be applied:

$$\Delta y_{i,t} = \beta_0 + \beta_1 \hat{y}_{i,t-1} + \beta_2 \Delta \hat{x}_{i,t} + \beta_3 d_{i,t} + E_{i,t} \tag{13}$$

Where $\Delta y_{i,t}$ is the current growth rate of real GRP per capita, 2000-2007; $\hat{y}_{i,t-1}$ is the lagged level of GRP per capita (endogenous); in (13.3) we also use lagged growth rate (endogenous); $\Delta \hat{x}_{i,t}$ is a vector of growth rates of control variables including real fixed investments per capita (endogenous), the share of employed population (endogenous), created technologies per capita (endogenous); $d_{i,t}$ is a vector of time dummies as in (13.2) (3 years for 2000-2006 and 1 for 2007) or as in (13.3) a vector of year dummies (exogenous); β are coefficients and $E_{i,t}$ is a composite error term: specific and idiosyncratic errors. For the system GMM estimation we use the endogenous growth rates of the control variables and instrument them (see explanations below). The only exogenous controls are the time period dummies.

The strategy for the dynamic analysis can be summarized as follows: first we estimate the model without the lagged levels of real GRP per capita by first differencing as in Wooldridge (2002, pp. 279-281) to eliminate unobserved effects. Then we add the lagged levels of real GRP per capita in (13.2) and lagged growth rates in (13.3) and apply a two-step system GMM estimation with the "xtabond2" package as in Roodman (2006) using Windmeijer's correction as in Windmeijer (2005) for errors and testing the overidentifiying restrictions with Sargan and Hansen tests. We will mainly rely on the Hansen test since it uses a heteroscedasticity consistent weighting matrix as stated in Chao et al. (2014, p. 8); however, we also report the Sargan test results and comply with the 5% level for both tests. For the system GMM, we have equation in levels for which differences are used as instruments and equation in differences for which levels are used as instruments as suggested in Arellano and Bover (1995, p. 48). Since we have 328 observations and 45 in (13.2) with period controls or 48 in (13.3) with year controls as instruments, it was essential to collapse the instrument matrix, otherwise the "xtabond2" issued a warning of too many instruments. Lagged level of GRP, investments, labour and new technologies are treated as endogenous, whereas time period dummies are exogenous. We test the residuals of our models (13.1), (13.2) and (13.3) on white noise with the Portmanteau test as in Montgomery et al. (2008, p. 57). This is considered to be a measure of fit for time-series models and can be well applied to dynamic panel data residuals. If the residuals are not white noise, then there might be hidden autocorrelation in idiosyncratic errors, so this test is decisive for the model quality.

Specification (13.1) is a simple estimation in First Differences (further FD) as in Wooldridge (2002, pp. 279). Since the time period is 2000-2007, we might assume some autocorrelation, so differencing is more preferable to averaging as in the Fixed Effects approach. As we see from the Table 6, FD performs well since residuals are white noise; however, adding a lagged dependent variable in differences or in levels would contradict the exogeneity assumption.

Working with the lagged levels and differences of the dependent variable requires the system GMM approach to instrument these lags. Therefore we treat all the variables in the equation as endogenous and period or year dummies as exogenous. Islam (1995, p. 1135) suggested a framework for deriving β-convergence from the coefficients on the lagged GDP (or GRP) per capita with a growth rate as a dependent variable. In (13.2) we include the lagged level of GRP per capita as it was done in Ledyaeva and Linden (2008, p. 94). According to Ledyaeva and Linden (2008, p. 95) this coefficient should not be directly interpreted as the speed of convergence. The coefficient on the lagged level of GRP from (13.2) is significant and shows that with 1% increase in lagged level of real GRP per capita, the growth rate in the following year decreases with a coefficient of -0.0554. As in Ledyaeva and Linden (2008, p. 95) we apply the additional calculation $-0.0554 = e^{-\lambda T}$ where $T = 5$, or 5 years, since we are interested in the convergence speed for each year. Therefore, λ, or the convergence speed (or β-convergence), is equal to 1.13% per year. This is a surprisingly small speed; however, as noted in Ledyaeva and Linden (2008, p. 95), the convergence speed measured in the dynamic framework is in general lower than the one obtained from the cross-section growth regressions. This is partly confirmed by the finding of Bond et al. (2001, p. 24), who find that system GMM coefficients are in general lower than the ones obtained by other techniques. The reason is clear: in system GMM we control for time and use growth rates for each year. This allows us to isolate the impact of time and exogenous events and shocks; however, we must bear in mind that convergence occurs through time and thus parts of the explanatory power and the coefficient magnitude will be drained by time dummies. This issue has not been sufficiently discussed in the empirical literature since the authors rarely combine and compare OLS cross-section regressions and dynamic panel data estimates.

We perform additional estimation (13.3) with dummies for every year 2000-2007 (2000 and 2007 were dropped out due to technical aspects of the Stata routines) and a lagged growth rate of real GRP per capita. Firstly, we should note that the coefficient on lagged growth is negative and significant on all levels even after controlling for each year. In specification (13.3) the transformation of the coefficient is not required and can interpret the result directly. Thus, a 1% growth rate would slower the subsequent growth rate by 0.170. Since $T = 5$ the convergence speed per year would be 2.98%. The coefficient is still small; however if we refer to Kufenko (2012, p. 12), and take the coefficient from specification (3) with collapsed instrumental matrix, 0.717, we could apply the Islam (1995, p. 1136)[10] formula and obtain the following relation $0.717 = e^{-\lambda T}$. Therefore, in Kufenko (2012, p. 12), the

[10] A technical note is necessary: Islam (1995, p. 1135 - 1136) uses different formulas: for the coefficient on the lagged level with growth as the dependent variable ($= e^{-\lambda T} - 1$) and for the coefficient on the lagged level with a dependent variable in levels ($= e^{-\lambda T}$).

Table 6. FD and two-step system GMM

	FD	Sys GMM two-step	
	(13.1)	(13.2)	(13.3)
VARIABLES	growth	growth	growth
$y_{i,t-1}$		-0.0554*	
		(0.0317)	
		-1.747	
$\Delta y_{i,t-1}$			-0.170***
			(0.0623)
			-2.737
inv	0.0901***	0.0916***	0.0901***
	(0.0167)	(0.0185)	(0.0165)
	5.400	4.949	5.457
lab	-0.169	-0.553	-0.549
	(0.359)	(0.744)	(0.546)
	-0.472	-0.744	-1.004
tech	0.00917	0.00262	0.00105
	(0.00642)	(0.00623)	(0.00674)
	1.427	0.420	0.156
third		-0.0703*	
		(0.0397)	
		-1.772	
fourth	-0.000337	-0.0300	
	(0.00924)	(0.0203)	
	-0.0365	-1.478	
fifth	0.00619		
	(0.0139)		
	0.446		
Constant	0.205***	0.850**	0.258***
	(0.0102)	(0.366)	(0.0209)
	20.20	2.324	12.35
Time dummies	periods	periods	2000-2007 dummies
Observations	328	328	328
Adj. R-squared	0.0849	-	-
Instruments	-	45	48
Prob > F (chi2)	0.0000	0.0000	0.0000
Homoskedasticity	0.1010	Windmeijer's correction	Windmeijer's correction
Residuals white noise test	1	1	1

Standard errors in parentheses
*** p<0.01, ** p<0.05, * p<0.1

Source: proprietary estimation

actual speed of convergence was 5.5% since $T = 6$, which is also relatively high. As mentioned previously, the estimates can be much lower: Firdaus and Yosup (2009, p. 81) report 0.29% for the speed of dynamic convergence in the regions of Indonesia. Firdaus and Yosup (2009, pp. 81-82) also find a large gap between OLS estimate of convergence and system GMM results. One should note once again, that the coefficients obtained depend on specification and time frames. We distinguish between the cross-section speed of convergence and the dynamic one.

Proposition 10. *The speed of β-convergence in the dynamic system GMM estimation varies from 1.13% and 2.98% to 5.5% per year in the estimations of the author (which is consistent with the cross-section estimates but is relatively low; however, Ledyaeva and Linden (2008, p. 95) also report a low value of 1.24% for dynamic convergence). In general, after controlling for time, the dynamic speed of convergence is lower than the estimate obtained after cross-section regressions.*

Bearing in mind that in the cross-section growth regressions the conditional β-convergence was ranging from 2.036 to 3.898%, we should note that both estimates originate from completely different dimensions and estimation techniques. Whereas the magnitudes of the speed of convergence significantly differ from each other; the negative sign and significance is a common feature of all our estimations.

Specifications (13.1), (13.2) and (13.3) leave residuals which are white noise or in other words represent serially uncorrelated, zero-mean, constant and finite variance process as in Hamilton (1994, pp. 47-48). The stationarity of residuals is not sufficient, since the white noise test checks whether the variance is constant: stationary residuals may not always be white noise; however, white noise residuals would always be stationary. Specification (13.2) performs well in all tests for the validity of the overidentifying restrictions, except the Sargan test, where the probability value is 0.051 which is marginally larger than 5%. Specification (13.3) has this value for the Sargan test around 0.17. Once again, we note that this Sargan test is not robust as stated in Chao et al. (2014, p. 8). The Hansen test probability value is 0.267 for specification (13.2) and 0.581 for (13.3). As we have previously mentioned, both tests, especially the Hansen test, may be sensitive to the number of instruments used. Keeping this fact in mind, we consider estimation results with caution. Test results are placed in the Appendix.

1.6 Summary of Chapter 1

After analyzing and simulating the basic Solow model, and considering its extensions, we established the main features of the model including σ-

and β-convergence, and highlighted the key determinants of growth: saving rate, technology, human capital and institutions. Due to the empirical nature of our research, we proceeded to a literature overview on methods applied to estimating economic growth with a focus on OLS growth regressions and system GMM approaches: this was essential to compare the magnitudes and signs of the coefficients obtained in our proprietary analysis. Afterwards, we described our datasets for OLS and system GMM models, and performed estimations. The OLS growth models for 1995-2007 involved initial and intermediate values of growth determinants and were tested on heteroscedasticity, specification errors and multicollinearity. Coefficients were obtained with outliers, without outliers and with weighted outliers (robust regression with Huber and bi-weighting).

Before conducting the analysis, we graphically showed the presence of β-convergence and the absence of σ-convergence for the time period of 1995-2007. The main empirical findings from the OLS growth regressions were the following: the annual speed of unconditional cross-section β-convergence was around 1.895% from specification (12.1) to the highest estimate of the annual speed of conditional cross-section β-convergence 3.898% from specification (12.5); fragile positive impact of real investments per capita around 1.534% from specification (12.2); fragile negative impact of the share of civil servants in the employed population of -1.057% of growth from specification (12.4); robust positive impact of the share of the employed population with higher education of 0.136% from specification (12.4) and 0.12% from the extended specification (12.7); fragile negative impact of the Carnegie Center democracy index of -0.124% from the extended specification (12.6) excluding outliers; robust negative decrease in growth by 0.370 for each additional 1000 kilometers distance from Moscow form the extended specification (12.7) with treated outliers. The OLS growth regressions have passed heteroscedasticity and omitted variable bias tests and yielded plausible VIF values.

Acknowledging the problem of "too many instruments", we reported the results of the two-step system GMM estimation consistent with autocorrelation tests, Sargan and Hansen tests and white noise test on residuals. The results suggest that in the dynamic framework, real investments per capita are a significant positive determinant of growth and the speed of convergence ranges from 1.13% to 2.98% from specifications (13.2 and 13.3), including 5.5% from the previous work of the author, Kufenko (2012, p. 12). The system GMM results should be considered with caution due to 45-48 instruments against 328 observations used, even though all the tests were passed. Endogenous and exogenous instruments are listed in the model specifications and tests statistics are reported in the Appendix.

2

The resource curse and human capital

Having confronted the neo-classical growth model with the data on the Russian regions, we now have to focus on the main issue for the Russian economy - the resource curse. The reason why the blessing with the natural resources may turn into a curse is extremely hard to capture with econometric techniques. Thus, we have to analyze the data on industrial structure and examine different causes of the resource curse. We will try to grasp the consequences of the resource curse in Russia with a special focus on the brain-drain problem. The resource curse is often associated with a lower demand for human capital - we will try to check this using the wage distribution. Afterwards we will model the hazardous impact of the resource curse on human capital with the help of game-theoretic approach. Since human capital proxy was relatively robust in some specification in the OLS growth regressions, we consider the human capital to be one of the most crucial, and yet, very vulnerable (e.g. because of the brain-drain), determinants of growth.

2.1 The resource curse: the Dutch disease and institutions

As in De Rosa and Iootty (2012, pp. 2-3) Russia is often considered a country experiencing a resource curse phenomenon (also known as the paradox of plenty). Let us focus more on this aspect and show how the resource abundance may impact on growth, institutions, and human capital. As stated in Leite and Weidmann (1999, p. 21) an abundance of natural resources in frames of the neoclassical growth model can be interpreted as a "positive technology shock", turning natural resources into a long-run positive determinant of economic growth. Leite and Weidmann (1999, p. 21) note at least two reasons which can turn the blessing into a curse: direct (Dutch disease) and indirect (institutions). Thus we will consider two main approaches to the given problem: the Dutch disease (related to changes in production structure and human capital) and institutions (rent-seeking behaviour). We will finalize the part on the resource curse with a game-theoretic illustration of the brain-drain problem.

Since Sachs and Warner (1995), the problem of economic growth under resource abundance has been widely discussed and researched. The hypothesis that countries experiencing abundance of natural resources would have lower economic growth rates than countries poor in such resources may at first glance appear confusing: in the 1960s after the work of Habakkuk (1962), it was believed that natural resource endowments act as catalyzers for economic growth. In addition, a trivial Ricardian comparative advantage logic, as in Costinot and Donaldson (2012), would lead us to a conclusion that countries specialize their production and trade structure according to their factor productivities and thus resource-abundant countries would tend to specialize in raw materials, whereas countries poor in resources, would specialize in other industries, for example manufacturing. In terms of the well-established Heckscher-Ohlin trade model, the resource curse can be associated with the Dutch disease described as follows: according to Rybczynski (1955, pp. 340-341) an increase in a certain factor endowment would lead to an increase in the output of corresponding goods. For example, an increase in natural resource endowments would cause the production of primary goods to increase, whereas the production of manufactured goods would fall, other things equal.

As it follows from the Table 7, the specialization is far more complicated. Some of the dominant oil producers, like the Netherlands, the US, Norway and Canada, have an extremely large share of high-tech exports in their total manufactured exports. While the US practically refrains from exporting fuels, using it instead for domestic economy, Norway and Canada have substantial exports of carbon fuels. Obviously, the resource abundance does not completely govern the specialization and economic development. Nevertheless, from Table 7 we see that the abundance of natural resources can also be related to lower shares of high-tech exports: obviously Kuwait, Saudi Arabia, Algeria and Nigeria are far better examples of raw material specialization. It may appear striking, but Kazakhstan has a higher share of fuel exports than Russia, and in addition a higher share of high-tech goods in manufactured exports. One should note that the issue of trade and production specialization is more complex than the simple Ricardian thinking. This table helps us to compare the export profile of Russia with the profiles of other oil and gas exporters: clearly, fuels are dominating in the export structure, whereas the high-tech share of the manufactured exports is relatively modest.

Let us focus on the issue of the resource curse and its impact on economic growth. It will be also important to consider the influence of the given phenomenon on institutions and human capital. As in Sachs and Warner (1997), it is empirically shown that countries with high raw resource intensities experience slower growth rates. Moreover, according to Sala-i-Martin (1997, pp. 181-182), proxies for resource abundance such as a high share of primary exports, are highly robust and as a variable in empirical models have a negative impact on growth. A few of the most quoted proxies of the resource curse are the following: indirect proxies, such as the share of raw resources in exports (or in GDP) as in Sachs and Warner (2001) and direct proxies, such as mining and reserve quantities of resources as in Sala-i-Martin and Subramanian (2013) or natural capital, for example land area as in Canuto and Cavallari (2012). In our growth regression we have applied quantities of oil and gas extraction per capita as a proxy for the carbon-based resource abundance. For the Russian regions we did not find a significant impact of this variable on growth rates between 1995 and 2007. Canuto and Cavallari (2012) suggest a methodology of evaluation of the natural capital levels, and also stress the fact that different countries may potentially reach the same income level, albeit by different means: taking advantage of the rich resource endowments or inducing technological progress. A most preferable result would be a mixture of both and minimization of the share of the natural capital in the overall wealth per capita. One should note that the negative correlation between growth rates and resource abundance has an endogenous nature: obviously, oil and gas reserves alone would not be the main reason for economic backwardness and the main question here would be why the blessing turns into a curse for some countries?

Let us examine the conventional Dutch disease explanation of the nature of the resource curse phenomenon and explain how the resource abundance shaped economic developments in Russia after year 2000.

The data prior to 2005 on the industry structure were disaggregated and are incompatible with the data after 2005 due to differences in industry composition in the Goskomstat reports. Nevertheless, even if we consider the data for 2000-2004, we find that the share of extracted resources to the total is relatively stable and the relation is on average 78% for manufactured to 22% for extracted resources. The argument of a price-induced resource curse has very weak empirical evidence for Russia, at least with reference to the time span of 2000-2011. A similar method was applied in Eberhardt and Teal (2013) who traced the structural change and shifts of the economies from an agricultural sector to other sectors in dynamics. In the case of structural change towards the resource sector, as Sachs and Warner (2001) would predict, we should have observed the rising share of the extraction sector

Table 7. Specialization in fuels and high-tech goods

Oil/Gas producers	2005	
	Share of high-tech goods in manufactured exports (%)	Share of fuels in merchandise exports (%)
Algeria	1.484	98.027
Angola*	no data	no data
Azerbaijan	1.0564	76.764
Canada	13.084	21.61
Iran	2.4871	82.611
Iraq	no data	96.445
Kazakhstan	11.291	70.618
Kuwait	0.1167†	94.599
Netherlands	30.89	7.3541
Nigeria	1.7†	97.896
Norway	16.094	67.686
Russian Federation	8.4375	61.774
Saudi Arabia	0.6689	90.936
United Arab Emirates	1.8715	57.791
United States	29.902	3.2743
Venezuela, RB	2.302	87.958

Data: top-15 oil producers according to the CIA Factbook, World Bank.
*Although Angola is one of the major oil producers, the exact data for recent periods were not available
† value for the last available period

Table 8. Sectoral structural change

Year	Production output	
	Manufactured (%)	Extracted (%)
2005	77.52	22.47
2006	78.2	21.8
2007	78.22	21.77
2008	78.664	21.33
2009	77.35	22.65
2010	78.35	21.6
2011	77.09	22.91

Data: Goskomstat, "Russian Industry", 2012

and shrinkage of manufacturing, which is clearly not the case. Nevertheless, a structural change can be detected in many dimensions. Let us examine the manufacturing sector alone, as in the Table 9.

When considering the structure of the manufacturing sector, we observe a clear positive trend in the share of the carbon derivative production sub-sector: from 2005 to 2011, even despite the global financial crisis and the consequent decrease in oil prices, the carbon derivative sub-sector grew from 16.2% to 19.9%.

Proposition 11. *In Russia the resource abundance is mainly characterized by the sub-sector shifts of manufacturing towards increasing the output of carbon derivatives; whereas the overall proportions of manufacturing to extraction are relatively stable.*

Table 9. Sub-sectoral structural change

Year	Manufacturing output Carbon derivatives (%)
2005	16.208
2006	17.899
2007	16.29
2008	17.694
2009	18.548
2010	18.62
2011	19.924

Data: Goskomstat, "Russian Industry", 2012

The importance of a sub-sector structural change is not often highlighted by authors; however, the sub-sector structural change and growth of the carbon derivative production sub-sector within the manufacturing sector in Russia is obvious. Thus, we state the presence of the sub-sector structural change in manufacturing, driven by the resource abundance, particularly in carbon resources. It is noteworthy that the structural change in economies of countries with resource abundance is rarely studied in the economic literature. Considering the economic nature of the resource curse, let us focus on the labour market.

Bearing in mind the above-mentioned sub-sector structural change, let us consider Sachs and Warner (2001) from a different angle: the Russian labour market and the potential impact of the resource abundance on human capital. The chart above indicates the relation of an industry-specific average wage to an overall average monthly wage of approximately 710 USD[11] in

[11] With the exchange rate of 31 RUB per 1 USD, as taken from the website of the Central Bank of Russia, www.cbr.ru

2010. An additional piece of information is required: in 2010, around 15.6% of employed population were working in the sphere of education, 12.8% were employed in the sphere of health-care and 3.1% were employed in hospitality services [12] . That makes 31.5% of the employed population receiving less than 0.75 of the average wage. According to press release N2297 of the WCIOM, approximately 27% of respondents in Russia in 2012 were not satisfied with their present job. In addition, 35% of the respondents in 2012 explicitly mentioned that they receive a low wage and were considering a job change[13]. The social attitudes confirm the presence of wage disparities. In contrast to education (0.67 of the average wage), resource extraction (2.21 of the average wage) and carbon derivative manufacturing (1.98 of the average wage) are sectors with much higher wages. It is interesting to note that only 0.9% of the employed population works in the resource extraction sector and enjoy wages twice higher than the average wage and three times higher than the average wage in education.

Proposition 12. *According to the sector-related wage distribution, in 2010, the highest wage premium over the average wage was observed in financial services, resource extraction and manufacturing of carbon derivatives, whereas the wages in education were only 0.67 of the average.*

We do not fully possess the data for a substantial cross-country comparison; however, in 2006, in Germany the average monthly wage was around 2 544 EUR, whereas the wage of different categories of researchers in education was between 3 233 and 3 699 EUR which is around 1.4 higher than the average[14].

In Russia the wage in education was only 0.67 of the average wage in 2010 and Figure 7 points out to other sharp contrasts. To be more precise, the average wage in education is 3.29 times lower than the average wage in resource extraction, according to the data of 2010. Such a premium over the average wage would not result in an immediate change of qualification. However, production factors would flow to industries with higher returns, and in this case, it is logical to assume that labour would flow to a sector with a higher wage. One should acknowledge that it is quite problematic for professors employed in education or research (both are considered to

[12] Goskomstat, "Russian annual statistics", 2012, section 5.5

[13] WCIOM press release 2297.
Available at: http://wciom.ru/index.php?id=459uid=114058

[14] According to: Verdienststrukturerhebung - durchschnittliche Bruttojahres-/Bruttomonatsverdienste der Arbeitnehmer/-innen nach ausgewaehlten Berufen.
Available at:
https://www.destatis.de/DE/Publikationen/Thematisch/VerdiensteArbeitskosten/

Fig. 7. Sector-related wage distribution (2010)

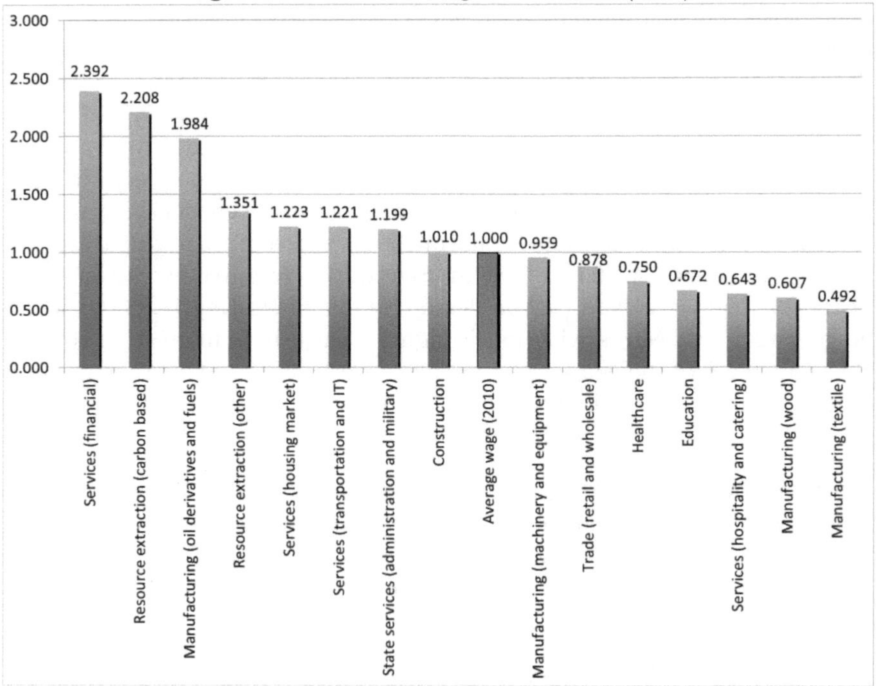

Data: Goskomstat

be identical in the Goskomstat database) to start working on an oil pump. Thus, those employed in education must consider other opportunities and at best, avoid changes in qualification. The labour market wage disparities are one of the reasons for the brain-drain, or the outflow of researchers from Russia to other countries. Let us consider the quantitative dynamics of the number of researchers related to oil price dynamics regarding two countries. For this consideration we have selected Germany since, as in Gathmann and Koch (2013)[15], 896 researchers from Russia were employed in Germany in 2010. Thus, Russians represent the majority of foreign researchers employed in Germany, at least for the year 2010. Keeping this fact in mind, we are able to only partly capture the scale of the brain-drain from Russia.

On the scatterplot below we observe an intriguing stylized fact: in Russia the number of researchers decreases; whereas in Germany it is the opposite. This observation is even more intriguing if we consider the dynamics of

[15] We have used the printed version of the article, a shorter version without tables is available online:
http://www.duz.de/duz-magazin/2013/02/auf-rubel-komm-raus/167

the oil prices. One could assume that the oil prices would simply represent the time dimension; however, there may be another explanation. One hypothetical reason for such developments is that in Russia, due to resource abundance, technology and energy-saving technology in particular has a lower priority, whereas in Germany, due to an absence of the resource abundance, technology and energy-saving technology in particular would have a higher priority.

Fig. 8. Brain-drain as a trend

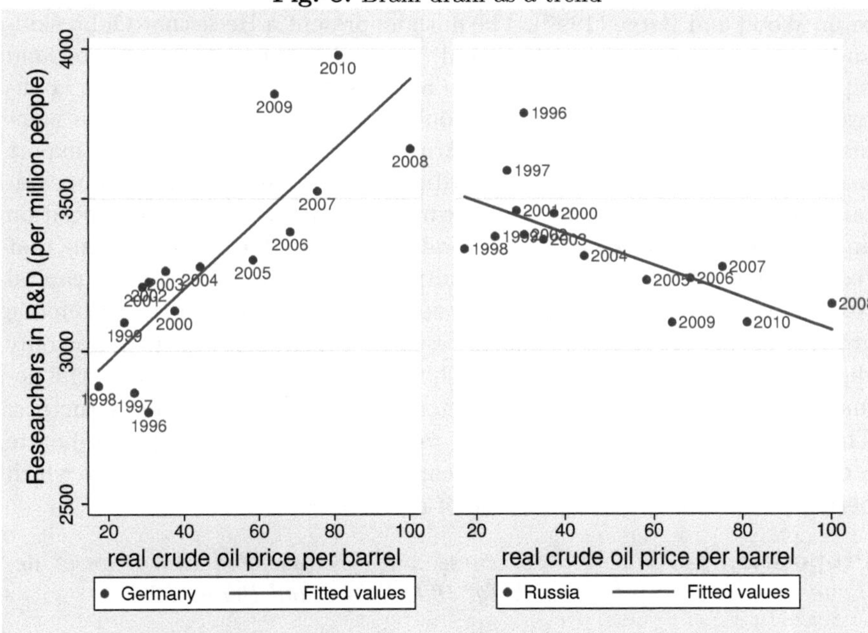

Data: World Bank, InflationData.com

Proposition 13. *In Russia the number of researchers has been steadily decreasing.*

This does not imply the reverse, and does not imply that there is a linear causal relation. One should regard this as a stylized fact since the oil prices can simply represent the flow of time. Nevertheless, we will try to expand on the above-mentioned explanation. It is possible that due to cost-saving behaviour, German entities may conduct more research, for example, of energy-saving technologies, whereas in Russia such research may be relevant only in the distant future, when the once abundant natural resources are exhausted. The movement of human capital would be in accord with the demand for research or the demand for this type of capital. Even though we refer to the cost-driven research explanation of the brain-drain, the resource curse, to our mind, is an integral element of these developments. Thus, for Russia, we establish that the resource abundance is one of the major causes of the labour market disparities and the brain-drain of human capital. The question as to why certain countries experience brain-drain and other countries brain-gain, or accumulate human capital, may be answered in a more detailed way, but this lies beyond the scope of our research.

One can find the link between the resource endowment and human capital in Wood and Berge (1997). The authors present a Heckscher-Ohlin skill-and-land-only model (see Wood and Berge, 1997, pp. 36-38) where land represents the natural resource. The authors empirically show that countries with high skill/resource ratio would tend towards specializing in manufactured goods, whereas countries with a low ratio would tend to export primary goods. In other words, according to the latter authors human capital relation to natural resource endowment governs the export composition and thus the trade specialization. Wood and Berge (1997, p. 35) assume that the manufacturing sector creates additional production and human capital related externalities which, according to the authors, contribute to economic growth. Auty (1998, p. 20) quotes research suggesting that it is not only the supply of human capital which should be analyzed, but rather the demand for human capital, which is determined by the production structure. The production-determined demand for human capital would also dictate a certain price, or return to human capital in a particular economy, which perhaps would be lower in the case of resource curse.

Proposition 14. *The resource curse may be associated with a lower demand for human capital (see Auty, 1998; Wood and Berge, 1997).*

Gylfason (2001, p. 16) discusses whether resource abundance is associated with lower investments, schooling, trade and higher corruption, which represents the mainstream conclusions, repeated by many, while some authors assume the contrary and claim that the resource curse is in fact a blessing: Cavalcanti et al. (2009, p. 20) take advantage of the panel of 53 and 27 years and find that the effect of oil abundance on real income is significantly positive. Cavalcanti et al. (2009, p. 9) explain the negative coefficient received by other researchers by an omitted variable bias and methodological aspects. After accounting for unobserved common shocks and common correlated effects they claim to receive a positive coefficient on oil abundance.

So far we have investigated the economic aspects of the resource curse. But some authors, including De Rosa and Iootty (2012, pp. 3-8), claim that resource abundance may impact on institutions and governance. The complexity of this interaction is related to the latent nature of institutions and institutional quality, which is difficult to measure accurately. Leite and Weidmann (1999) focus on the emergence of a rent-seeking behaviour in resource abundant countries. The authors refer to Romer (1994a, pp. 23-25) where, using the "Dupuit's equilibrium", a clear-cut comparison of corruption with an informal "bridge-crossing" fee is made. Needless to say, both are considered as trade restrictions, severely damaging the domestic welfare. Romer (1994a) argues that such trade restrictions hinder economic growth. Consequently, Leite and Weidmann (1999, p. 5) suggest a deeper understanding of the institutional aspects of the resource curse: resource abundance stimulates rent-seeking behaviour, which in turn increases corruption. The latter hinders economic growth and investments, and functions as an additional tax levied on firms and their profits. However, corruption is more distortionary and costly than taxation, as presented in Shleifer and Vishny (1993, p. 614). Another logical explanation of the institutional aspect of the resource curse is that rent-seeking behaviour opposes entrepreneurship or productive activities, as can be found in Torvik (2002).

Proposition 15. *Resource abundance may promote rent-seeking behaviour and corruption as well as other inefficient institutions (see De Rosa and Iootty, 2012; Leite and Weidmann, 1999).*

One has to note that the resource abundance may not necessarily promote the rent-seeking behaviour. Each country has an institutional matrix, which has been shaped by a certain historical path. This is also applied to Russia as stated in Hedlund (2005, p. 15), where "kormlenie"[16] is mentioned as a legally defined mean of sustaining civil servants and militia at the cost of local population. In 15th century Russia this method was widespread and regional authorities were entitled to "feed" from the local population without any limits, as in Hedlund (2005, p. 15). Therefore, the rent-seeking behaviour may already be integrated in the institutional matrix and discovery of oil or gas would only stimulate the existing inefficient institution of rent-seeking.

We now have a better understanding that the resource curse may have a negative impact on growth not only due to the structural change, labour market disparities and a lowering human capital demand, but also due to a lowering institutional quality and increasing corruption, driven by the rent-seeking behaviour. Needless to say, as in Mo (2001, p. 76), corruption reduces economic growth. In meta-analysis, as in Ugur and Dasgupta (2011, p. 30), the negative impact of corruption on growth is highlighted consistently.

[16] In Russian: feeding or nourishing.

Investigating the resource curse is an essential and integral part of our research. Considering the causes and consequences of the resource abundance in Russia, we can establish that a sub-sector structural change and growth of the carbon derivative production sub-sector within manufacturing took place during 2005-2011, labour market and wage disparities resulted in the fact that in 2010 around 0.9% of the employed population work in the extraction sector and receive 2.21 of the average wage, whereas 31.5% of the employed population work in healthcare, education, hospitality and several other sectors and receive less than 0.75 of the average wage and three times less than the average wage in the extraction sector[17]; we have established a negative trend in the number of researchers in Russia, and were able to partly capture the brain-drain phenomenon confirming a hazardous impact of the resource abundance on human capital. An insight in the institutional aspect of the resource curse and an overview of the related literature hints at the fact that resource abundance promotes rent-seeking behaviour and thus increases corruption. The latter hinders growth, investments and dampens entrepreneurship. These findings will be used in the further parts of our research, particularly when dealing with income distribution and its relation to the recent protests in Russia.

In the next part of our work we will try to focus on the brain-drain problem and show the decision-making processes of the human capital bearer and the state as an investor in human capital. With the help of the game theory design we will show that the resource curse can be extremely dangerous for human capital.

2.2 A game-theoretical approach to the brain-drain problem

Since Lucas (1988) and Mankiw et al. (1992) human capital has often been included in the new-classical Solowian growth model as an explanatory variable. The debates on the exogeneous *versus* endogeneous nature of human capital as well as the best empirical proxies are still relevant. The number of theoretical and empirical papers that consider human capital in frames of the neo-classical growth model is impressive, but only few researchers have examined the problems of human capital from different angles. A game-theory approach, as applied in Wu (2007) to model the corporate human capital investment decision-making process, would be a good example of such unorthodox methodology. In our opinion, this approach

[17] Data: Goskomstat, "Russia in Figures", Available:
http://www.gks.ru/wps/wcm/connect/rosstat_main/rosstat/ru/statistics/

would enable us to discuss two main human capital related issues for Russia: the brain-drain and human capital investment decision-making.

Let us consider a decision-making game with a player, bearer of human capital and the environment, the state. In a very simple case, the researcher would have two strategies: stay in the pool of researchers or change by exiting the pool of researchers. As for the second decision we should note that leaving the pool of researchers for a different occupation would cause diminution of human capital, no matter what the new occupation is: a foreign pool of researchers in a different country or a different profession in the home country. Thus, the decision to change is automatically associated with the brain-drain: human capital bearers leaving the pool of domestic researchers would decrease the aggregate level of human capital in the country of origin.

Let us define the key functions in a narrative way. For changing, the researcher gets a payoff:

$$C = w(1 + z) + k \tag{14}$$

Where C is the payoff for changing, w is the current real wage, z is the pecuniary reward for changing (can be seen as a bonus over the wage), k is a non-pecuniary reward for changing, for example a better institutional environment.

The introduction of the non-monetary aspect of the brain-drain decision is explained by numerous facts from biographies of famous Nobel prize winners, for example as in Hagemann (2010), the story of Wassily Leontieff, who migrated from the Soviet Union to Germany, and then to the US. From the biography of Wassily Leontieff it follows that the researcher was not only pursuing a higher wage, but rather was pushed by the forming institutional environment. For example, originating from a rich, bourgeois family (as in the case of Wassily Leontieff) would bring about certain problems and risks in the young Soviet Russia, where the proletariat was considered the dominant ruling class of the new society. The migration of Wassily Leontieff to Germany took place shortly after several police investigations against his university fellows, who faced purely ideological charges. Another related fact is the migration of Sergey Guriev, a famous Russian economist, who had to leave Russia in 2013 due to political reasons, or Sergey Aleksashenko. In such cases, the monetary aspect would hardly play a role in the decision-making. One should note that these non-monetary factors can be very specific and would vary from one individual to another. In contrast, in the case of staying in the pool of researchers, the environment comes into play with two possible states: an increase of the real wage with a probability of p and a situation, when the increase does not occur with the probability $1 - p$. The payoffs are assigned accordingly:

$$V^{\lambda>0} = w(1+\lambda) + n \ \ and \ \ V^{\lambda=0} = w + n \tag{15}$$

Where λ is a pecuniary reward and n is the non-pecuniary reward for staying.

Fig. 9. Brain-drain game tree

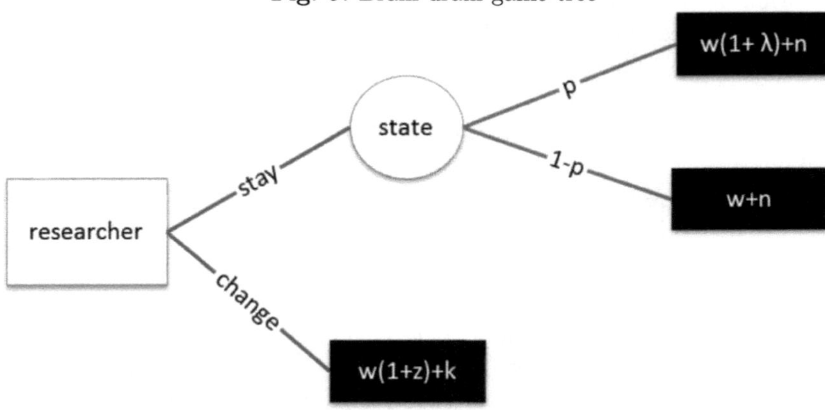

Source: proprietary

We proceed by comparing expected utilities and formulate and expand the change condition, the Δ:

$$\begin{aligned} \Delta &= pV^{\lambda>0} + (1-p)V^{\lambda=0} - C \\ \Delta &= p\big(w(1+\lambda)+n\big) + (1-p)(w+n) - \big(w(1+z)+k\big) \\ \Delta &= w(p\lambda - z) + (n-k) \end{aligned} \tag{16}$$

Obviously, from Δ it follows that the decision to change would occur when $\Delta < 0$, and if $\Delta \geq 0$[18] the researcher decides to stay. If the weighted monetary bonus for staying and the monetary bonus for leaving are the same, then the main role would be given to the non-monetary differential between staying and changing. Given the partial derivatives $\partial\Delta/\partial(w,\lambda,n) > 0$ and $\partial\Delta/\partial(z,k) < 0$ we can establish that the decision of the human capital bearer to stay or change does not solely depend on monetary bonuses: non-monetary bonuses or institutional environment can be at least as important

[18] One should bear in mind that leaving the domestic pool of researchers can be associated with costs.

for the decision-making.

This trivial apparatus of decision-making could be improved by adding dynamics and discounting. One could also introduce an uncertainty in the reward for changing. However, this is not needed, since this refinement would not change the intuitive conclusions: the bearer of human capital compares the monetary and non-monetary rewards of staying in the pool of researchers or leaving it under information uncertainty, since he/she does not know whether staying will be rewarded. In the case of homogeneous wages, the non-monetary factor would prevail and *vice versa.*

If we apply numeric simulation using the data from the wage distribution in Figure 7, providing the institutional environment is the same, then the human capital bearer, or the researcher, would most likely decide to choose an occupation closer to the average wage, that is to leave the pool of researchers who are paid around 0.67 of the average (if the present occupation lies within education). However, the human capital bearer can also leave the domestic pool of researchers for the foreign one. In most West-European countries the wage-gap would favor leaving the domestic pool of researchers. Of course, if we consider a heterogeneous pool of researchers with various positions or locations, the conclusion may be slightly different, but the logic of the model would remain valid.

Thus, in frames of the brain-drain game, the resource curse is nothing but a special set of conditions unpleasant for the human capital bearer. The existence of the resource curse would ensure that $z > \lambda$ according to proposition 14, due to lack of demand for human capital and $k > n$ according to proposition 15, due to corruption or other institutional distortions. Under these conditions the shift from the domestic pool of researchers is guaranteed.

Proposition 16. *Under the conditions associated with the resource curse, in frames of the brain-drain game, the human capital bearer is likely to leave the domestic pool of researchers.*

Naturally there are other factors which have not been considered in this simple decision-making model. Thus we note that proposition 16 is only valid with respect to the above-mentioned equations.

Let us divert from the previous game and focus on the decision-making on the macroeconomic level. For this we need to introduce a new set of functions. Assuming the state invests in the education of a future researcher, bearing in mind that the brain-drain problem is relevant. At the time of the decision-making the state does not know whether the future researcher would leave the pool of researchers or stay in it. Thus, for the state the researcher can be loyal with probability p and disloyal with probability $1 - p$. The game-design would be different: in this case we start with an information uncertainty. If the researcher remains loyal, the payoff of human capital investment is:

$$HC(1 + \pi) - I \tag{17}$$

Where HC is the present level of human capital, π is the return to investment in terms of human capital, I is the investment.

$$HC(1 - v) - I \tag{18}$$

Where HC is the present level of human capital, v[19] is the loss or diminution of human capital in case of leaving, I is the investment.

Needless to say, investments would be lost. An opposite strategy to investing is when the state simply ignores the researcher. If the researcher is disloyal, human capital would be diminished $HC(1-v)$ but the investments would be spared.

If the state believes that with 0.9 probability the researcher would be disloyal, then the optimal strategy would be to ignore the investment opportunity. Thus a continuous brain-drain game resulting in researchers leaving their occupation would sustain the belief that most of the researchers are disloyal. This belief would prevent the state from investing. If we assume that the state's investment I is related to w from equation (15), then a vicious circle is created: the researchers leave because the state does not invest in human capital, and the state does not invest because it expects researchers to leave. Modeling such a vicious circle would be problematic, so we do not interlink these two games. However, the hypothetical relation of I to w makes the state decision-making extremely important. The investments may not only be performed in a form of investments in education of a human capital bearer, but also in a form of grants or rise of salaries. Therefore, $w = f(I)$[20], or an assumption, that the wage of a researcher is a function of the state investments in human capital is plausible. This will be reflected in proposition 17.

Formalization of the state decision-making considering human capital is simple. The payoff of investing under information uncertainty of whether the future researcher is loyal or disloyal is the following:

$$V^{invest} = p\big(HC(1 + \pi) - I\big) + (1 - p)\big(HC(1 - v) - I\big) \tag{19}$$

Where where V^{invest} is the expected utility of investing and p is the probability that the researcher is loyal, whereas $1-p$ is the probability that the researcher is disloyal.

[19] One has to note that π and v do not have to be identical. Therefore, the return to investment in case of staying can be smaller than the diminution of human capital in case of leaving.

[20] One can assume that the wage of researchers can be also obtained from private sources: e.g., if the given person is employed in private research and development sphere. However, this would be less relevant for the sphere of education.

Fig. 10. Investing in human capital under the brain-drain

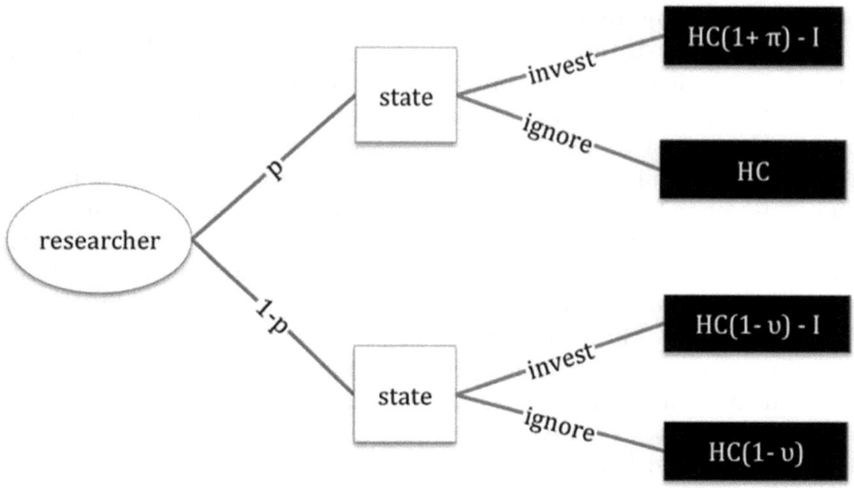

Source: proprietary

The payoff of ignoring the investment opportunity can be formulated as follows:

$$V^{ignore} = p(HC) + (1-p)\big(HC(1-v)\big) \tag{20}$$

Where where V^{ignore} is the expected utility of ignoring the investment opportunity and p is the probability that the researcher is loyal, whereas $1-p$ is the probability that the researcher is disloyal.

A separate sub-game equilibrium analysis yields that, in case of a loyal researcher the state will always invest in education, whereas if the researcher is beleived to be disloyal, the state will always ignore the investment opportunity, but this is obvious. The key problem is the critical probability p^* as in Carmichael (2005, p. 172): the state compares the actual probability with the critical one in order to decide whether the investment will occur. Let us start from the assumption that investment occurs when $V^{invest} > V^{ignore}$[21]. Then this condition can be reformulated:

$$p\big(HC(1+\pi)-I\big)+(1-p)\big(HC(1-v)-I\big) > p\big(HC\big)+(1-p)\big(HC(1-v)\big) \tag{21}$$

The critical probability would be then defined as:

$$p^* = \frac{I}{HC(\pi - 2v)} \tag{22}$$

[21] Here we assume strict inequality because investments can be associated with transaction costs.

Where p^* is the critical probability. In addition, we need to impose a restriction on the critical probability: $p^* \in [0; 1]$. Otherwise, the decision will not take place. In extreme cases when the critical probability is one of the border values, 0 or 1, the decision will be equivalent to the sub-game decision, providing that the actual probability coincides with the critical value. If the actual probability of a researcher being loyal is greater than then an investment will take place. However, if the actual probability is smaller than the critical value, the investment will not occur. The actual probability is associated with observed data or derived from it: for example, in 2013, according to a sociological questionnaire held by the "Levada Center" approximately 45% of students indicate that they want to emigrate from Russia[22]. There are numerous reasons for such responses, especially considering the first game theory model, although this result reflects a belief or a sequence of game theory outcomes with a certain subjective weighting. One could conclude, that this approach to the brain-drain allows us to consider it as an institution, as stated in Aoki (2001, pp. 26, 47-50), hazardous for some countries and beneficial for others. Linking these two games by an assumption that we may formulate the following proposition:

Proposition 17. *Under the conditions of the resource curse, a series of outcomes as in proposition 16, would create a belief of disloyal researchers which would discourage state investments into human capital, starting a vicious circle.*

This game demonstrates that beliefs are extremely important in the decision-making process. This partly explains the empirical fact that in Russia the expenditures in education have been fluctuating for a long time. The situation prior to 2007, when we observed a small increase in these expenditures, can be partly explained by a belief that human capital bearers are likely to be affected by the brain-drain.

To conclude, let us map the cumulative migration outflow from Russia and the number of researchers per million people. The cumulative migration outflow demonstrates a decreasing pace, with the number of researchers declining steadily as cumulative migration outflow grows. This may not mean that the diminution of human capital is solely attributed to migration, but we must note that there is a deep economic relationship between these two series - the brain-drain as explained by the means of the game theory approach, as referring to propositions 16 and 17.

There are several policy implications which follow from the abovementioned analysis: Firstly, government policies should aim at minimizing the negative economic and institutional consequences of the resource curse[23]

[22] Available at: http://top.rbc.ru/society/06/06/2013/860837.shtml

[23] Direct stimulation of the domestic manufacturing sector would be limited due to World Trade Organization legislation.

Fig. 11. Expenditure per student in tertiary education

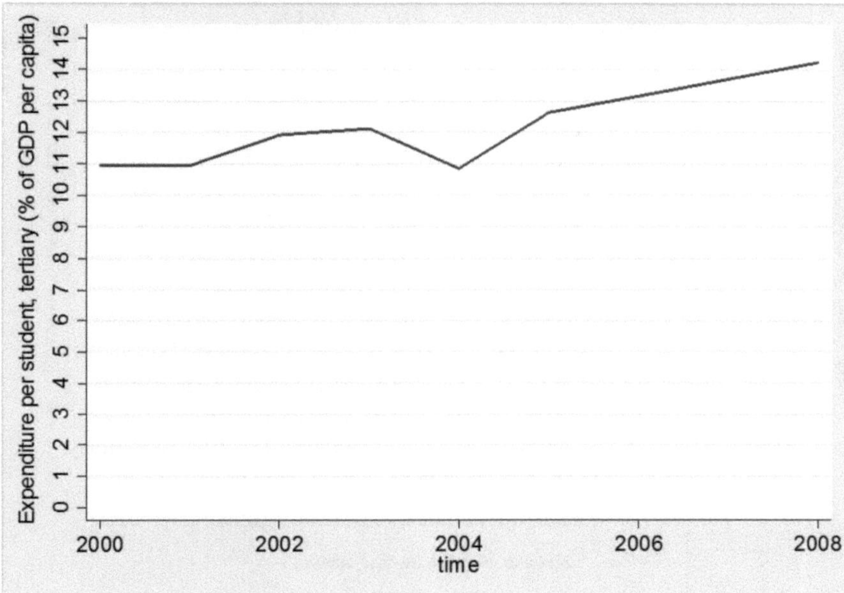

Data: World Bank, 2007 value linearly interpolated

by stimulating the demand for human capital in the long run. Secondly, improving the institutional environment is a necessary condition for promoting human capital[24] . In order to mitigate the uncertainties concerning investments in human capital, the government should offer more targeted grants and specify conditions of funding. These implications will be expanded in the conclusion.

[24] Current government policies in this sphere are controversial, for example, in 2010 a church was constructed on the territory of the National Research Nuclear University (or MEPhI) in Moscow and in 2012 the administration of the was forced to open a department of theology which caused numerous internal conflicts inside of the university and many researchers had to leave their positions. The reason for the conflicts was the fact that the church as well as the theology department were financed by the MEPhI administration, whereas many professors did not approve this fact. Such situations are described in Knox and Mitrofanova (2014, p. 47) as "creeping clericalization". In the mean time, projects such as "Skolkovo" are designed to promote scientific progress and stimulate demand for human capital.

Fig. 12. Cumulative migration and researchers per million people

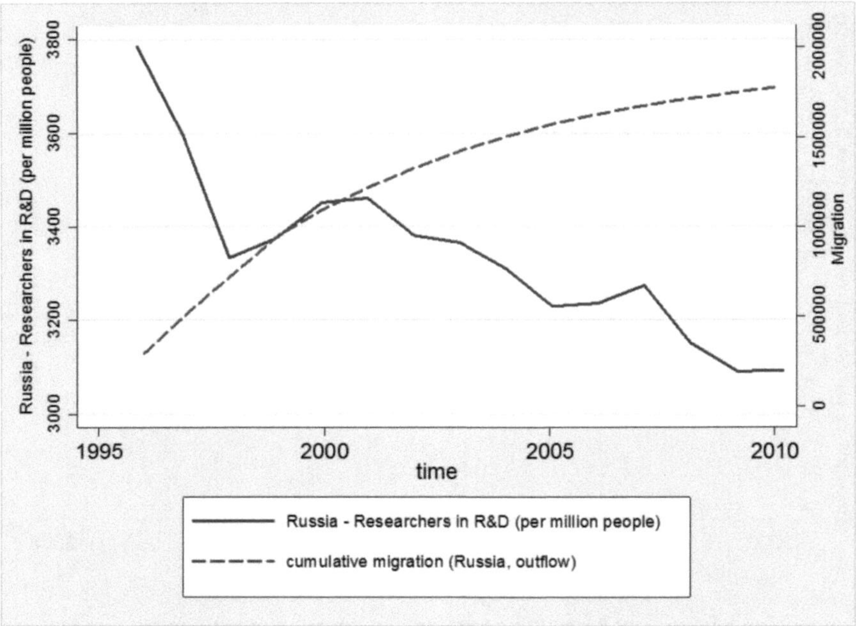

Data: World Bank, Goskomstat

2.3 Summary of Chapter 2

Considering the fact that the resource curse is one of the main problems to economic growth in Russia, we focused our attention on this issue. Bearing in mind that according to the data of Chapter 1, oil and gas extraction per capita did not have a significant coefficient, we decided to change the methodology and investigated the sectoral and sub-sectoral change in the Russian economy since 2005 (due to availability of the data). We found that the proportions of extraction to manufacturing are relatively constant; however, we detected a sub-sectoral shift: since 2005 the share of fuels in manufacturing has increased from 16 to 19.9%. We explored the economic and institutional interpretations of the resource curse including the Dutch disease, regulatory capture and rent-seeking behaviour, which are the dominant interpretations in the existing literature. Acknowledging the importance of the historical path dependence, we noted that the resource abundance may not necessarily promote the rent-seeking behaviour; however, if the rent-seeking behaviour is already integrated in the institutional matrix, the likelihood of a blessing with natural resources turning into a curse would increase. In addition, we discussed the demand for human capital under resource abundance, examine the wage differentiation emphasizing that the wages in education in 2010 were around 0.67 of the average wage (with one of the highest wages in resource extraction and fuel manufacturing occupations), and establish a negative trend in researchers per million population in Russia overlaying it on cumulative migration. Acknowledging the brain-drain problem, due to the absence of empirical data, we applied game theory to model the decision-making of human capital bearers and the state. One of the main theoretical findings is that human capital bearers decide whether they stay in the domestic pool of researchers or switch by comparing their monetary and non-monetary (e.g. institutional) payoffs. The resource curse can be formulated as a set of conditions, under which the human capital bearer will most likely leave the domestic pool of researchers. A flow of related game outcomes will form and a certain belief will establish. This will lead to a vicious circle since this belief will impact on the decision-making process of the state regarding the investments in human capital. Thus, the resource curse poses a great threat to human capital and a potential threat to long-term growth in Russia.

3

Economic Growth and Income Distribution

Having considered the determinants of economic growth and discussed the impact of the resource curse on human capital, we now have to proceed to the core topic of our research: income growth and income inequality. The main question is not only what drives economic growth, but whether it is fairly distributed. To avoid misunderstanding, we have to state that in our work economic growth is associated with income growth considering macro-economic understanding of the aggregate output. This is reasonable, since Kuznets (1955) uses the same understanding of income, which will be mentioned further. Acknowledging the complexity and non-linearity of the relation between growth and distribution, in Chapter 3 we will link economic growth and income distribution with the help of the well-established political Kuznets curve, pointing out the existence of revolution constraints based on income inequality. Then we will proceed to an empirical analysis of the determinants of the recent protests in 2011-2012 on a regional level with the latent variable model. By using different proxies for income inequality we will show that it is a significant and robust variable in predicting the risk of protests.

From the literature mentioned in Chapter 1 it is clear that the observed increase in gross regional product in Russia is dramatic. The question of the determinants of growth can be nowadays partially answered: federal and regional policies, physical and human capital, introduction of new technologies, institutions and historical or geographical background and other factors contribute to economic growth with different elasticity coefficients. The main intrigue of growth empirics is the magnitude of these coefficients. Keeping this in mind, one can ask a question: if income growth takes place, how is it distributed? Who benefits from it or, to rephrase, do all benefit equally? We have already mentioned regional disparities in Chapter 1 and it is reasonable to draw our interest to the issues of income distribution and inequality. In addition, one would require a different theoretical framework and establish a reasonable link between growth and income distribution.

One of the first attempts to postulate an interaction between income growth and inequality can be found in Kuznets (1955). Since then empirical and theoretical aspects of this interaction has been a subject of debates. The idea that income growth has a dynamic concave relation to income inequality - first, income growth triggers an increase in income inequality via production factor shift among sectors during industrialization, then, in the later stages of industrialization, the inequality will diminish and thus income growth will have an opposite effect on the inequality - was picked up by Acemoglu and Robinson (2002), who introduced a new element to it: the Median Voter Theorem (further, MVT). This resulted in a successful merger of political science and growth theory, providing a new political intuitive reasoning to the Kuznets curve.

Having considered the Kuznets curve on a macroeconomic scale, we will proceed to investigating the determinants of the recent protest which took place in Russia. We will thus try to find out whether the MVT explained Kuznets curve holds for the given countries and whether income inequality is a significant and robust determinant of the recent protests. The latter question will be answered with the help of logistic regressions ensuring plausible results by including a broad range of control variables.

Chapter 3 is organized as follows: in the first section we will discuss the implications of the MVT based political Kuznets curve and reformulate the income - income inequality scenarios, stated in Acemoglu and Robinson (2002). We will discuss the role of the revolution constraint and inequalities in human capital and wealth. In the second section we will focus on Russia and briefly examine the stylized facts at the regional level. The last section will be focused on empirical analysis of the determinants of the recent protest: we will test the role of income inequality proxies in predicting the probability of protests. In the summary we will present the results of our findings.

3.1 Literature overview: economic growth and income distribution

The Kuznets curve provides theoretical ground for our research. In order to understand how the given theory evolved, we have to consider the original formulation of the given theoretical relation. Kuznets (1955) was one of the first prominent economists to postulate the complicated relation of economic growth and income inequality. Noting the importance of distribution of income and savings, he related the changes in income inequality to the shifts of the industrial structure of income, the latter being a consequence of industrialization and economic growth.

One might be shocked by the intuitive and nevertheless detailed explanation of the relation between income and income inequality, which Simon Kuznets offered already in 1955, based on fragmented historical data from the UK, the US and Germany and an illustrative numerical model. Let us stepwise review the original reasoning for the Kuznets curve.

First of all, Kuznets (1955) refers to national income, the closest proxy to it is in fact gross national product (GNP) or, potentially, gross domestic product (GDP), since he deliberately specifies the term "national income". He also refers to secular levels of income (income distribution), which can be represented by different income inequality measures, including but not limited to Gini coefficient and income ratios. Kuznets highlights that an impulse of industrialization leads to urbanisation and shifts of production from agricultural sector to other industries. According to Kuznets (1955), the initial increase of income inequality is accounted for by an increase of income of urban population relative to the income of rural population. On the later phases of industrialization, the growing urban population will strive to smoothen the inequalities which would results in a decrease of disparities on a national scale. The narrowing of income inequalities as in Kuznets (1955) depends on the number of political and institutional factors: savings accumulation of the rich is subject to distributional reforms, democratization increases the role of low-income population groups, migration from rural areas to cities enables rural workers to work in industries with higher income. The increase of income inequalities due to structural changes in the economy is quite clear; however, a consequent process of narrowing of inequalities is conditional on at least several institutional factors. The original formulation for the levelling mechanism which could hypothetically decrease the income inequality with time lacks detail. Nevertheless, it offered room for new suggestions including a deeper consideration of political factors, which could narrow the above-mentioned inequalities.

In order to understand how the Kuznets curve evolved from an economic concept to a theory with a political background, we have to focus on the MVT and its implications. One of the first economists who started working on the topic of political competition was Harold Hotelling. Exploiting the homogeneity of political parties, Hotelling (1929) applies game-theoretic approach and finds striking similarities between competition in businesses and politics: in both cases, producers or political parties try to attract the majority of customers or voters, which explains the observed standardisation of products and political programmes. In order to perceive their goal, political parties focus on the interests of a representative voter - a voter, which represents the majority of voters. Black (1948) coins the term "median optimum", related to the decision-making process, which completes the Hotelling (1929) concept and allows us to identify the representative voter as a median voter. Downs (1957) can be considered as the most complete formulation of the MVT in its modern understanding. The key implications of the theoretical postulates of Downs (1957) can be described as follows: political decisions impact on income sources and, thus, income distribution; normal distribution of voters is essential for stability of the state, whereas polarization increases the risks of radical changes; multi-modal distribution of voters and political pluralism (multiparty system) are preferable. These key assumptions have formed solid grounds to further integration of MVT and its elements into the Kuznets curve. If we recall, the original formulation of the relation between income and income distribution did not account for politics of the decision-making process in regard to income distribution.

Bearing in mind that in general, MVT is related to political aspects of optimal taxation and distribution between at least two different income groups (usually, rich and poor), one has to admit that the scope of this concept is impressive. First of all, the MVT can be applied to study democratic processes and political competition as in Congleton (2004). It is also widely applied as a theoretical ground for examining taxation and provision of private goods as in Cornes and Sandler (1986, pp. 489-499) or Luelfesmann (2007). In addition, MVT implications are often used in economic growth research: McGuire and Olson (1996) state that in autocracies an optimal distribution is hard to achieve due to misuse of power; Alesina and Rodrik (1994) have shown that high levels of inequality are associated with lower economic growth. Even though that MVT has its roots in the political competition of the democratic and republican parties in the US, it can also be used as a platform for research of non-democratic processes and non-democratic regimes, e.g. autocracies: Acemoglu and Robinson (2006, Chpt. 6) is focused on applying the MVT apparatus to formulate a revolution constraint based on income ratios of the rich and the poor. One has to note that modelling non-democratic processes, especially political processes under non-tyrannical autocracies as in Boix and Svolik (2007), requires a more sophisticated game-theoretic approach than standard equations with tax distribution. Since we have briefly mentioned the revolution constraint, Bolle and Sahli (2007) is another example of research on autocratic regimes: the authors focus on impatience of the people and state that the performance and survival of the regime are subject to this impatience. Despite the criticism of the MVT, e.g. Scervini (2012), who argues that the role of the middle class in redistributive decision-making is fading away, we consider the given concept to be a solid ground[25] for examining the recent

[25] There are empirical studies, suggesting the robustness of the political Kuznets curve over the economic one (see Tam, 2008).

economic and political developments in Russia. It is also important to note, that MVT assumes a certain degree of political pluralism and competition, progressive tax rates and differentiated transfers (as well as different types of public goods) are also crucial for the given concept as in Winer and Hettich (2004, pp. 176-178).

Let us consider the political Kuznets curve with an integrated MVT element as in Acemoglu and Robinson (2002): a model of inequality dynamics, where the decisive role is given to the physical and human capital accumulation. We will refrain from a detailed presentation of the well-established model; however, we will highlight the setup, key equations and implications - the latter are crucial for the empirical part of our research.

First of all, Acemoglu and Robinson (2002) establish a two-player (the elite and the poor) multi-period game with generations and bequests to demonstrate accumulation of capital (human capital is considered to be a major asset). In the first period, the bequest decision regarding human capital is made and bequests are received, in the second period the elite decides whether they share the political franchise with the poor or not, in the third period the poor decide whether to revolt or not, fourth period denotes a new phase of bequest decisions and human capital accumulation. In fact, one can see this game as a line of cycles based on power-sharing and distribution through time. There are 3 cases of accumulation equations in Acemoglu and Robinson (2002) which we need to explicitly consider (see below) in order to understand the developmental scenarios in regard to the Kuznets curve.

First case is the autocracy where only the rich accumulate. In this case the steady state human capital level of the society will be the following as in Acemoglu and Robinson (2002, p. 192):

$$h_{ss} = \left((\gamma A)^{\beta} Z\right)^{1/(1-\beta)} \tag{23}$$

Where h_{ss} is a steady state level of human capital, A is an efficiency parameter, γ is a constant saving rate, Z is the offspring's initial level of human capital, β is a coefficient. In this case, the measure of inequality in the given society would be the income ratio of the rich to the poor as in Acemoglu and Robinson (2002, p. 192):

$$\frac{y_t^r}{y_t^p} = \frac{Ah_t^r}{A} = h_t^r \tag{24}$$

Where y_t is the income at time point t, h_t is the human capital level at time point t and r and p are the subscripts for the rich and the poor. In this case the steady state of the income would be defined as:

$$Y_{ss}^1 = A\Big(\lambda + (1-\lambda)\left((\gamma A)^{\beta} Z\right)^{1/(1-\beta)}\Big) \tag{25}$$

Where λ is the proportion of the poor agents. Therefore the poor will not be able to accumulate capital and thus the inequalities will increase through time. Second case is an autocracy where the rich and the poor accumulate:

$$Y_{ss}^2 = A\Big(\big((\gamma A)^{\beta} Z\big)^{1/(1-\beta)}\Big) > Y_{ss}^1 \tag{26}$$

In case of mutual accumulation, the economy will converge to a more equal distribution of income as in Acemoglu and Robinson (2002, p. 193). Obviously, in this situation the aggregate income is larger than in the first case (25) of extreme inequality.

Third case, with Y_{ss}^3, is a democracy where the tax rate is set by the median voter from the poor group. Here Acemoglu and Robinson (2002) state that only under additional conditions the poor will be able to accumulate capital[26]: firstly, the redistributive taxation should be sufficient to enable them to accumulate; secondly, the after-tax income of the poor multiplied by the savings rate is larger than 1. The crucial role of a democratic regime for the existence of the political Kuznets curve is further emphasized: capital accumulation and an increase of the income of the rich would mean an increase in income inequality; however, if this increase is followed by an optimal taxation and redistribution schemes, introduced by the will of the poor median voters, this would result in catching up of the poor and a decrease of inequalities.

Obviously, according to equation (26), the aggregate output when both rich and poor accumulate is higher than in an extreme case when only the rich accumulate; however, in other cases the situation may not be so clear. From Acemoglu and Robinson (2002, 2006) it follows that the relation between growth and distribution is non-linear and would depend on institutional and political background. Therefore, we refrain from an empirical analysis of the impact of income inequality on growth or *vice versa*. Econometric techniques would be biased due to reverse causality and endogeneity. Even if we attempt to treat these issues, we still might not be able to capture the true effect. For the sake of our research, we will take the arguments of Barro (2000, pp. 5-7): capital market imperfections; inequality in human capital (inequality in human capital may also lead to limited access to credit), corruption and fraudulent elections and social unrest. Nevertheless, Barro (2000, p. 8) refers to special cases of transition economies and notes that inequality may drive growth since the rich might have higher propensity to save and thus to invest. Barro (2000, p. 29) finds

[26] Providing that the poor are unable to accumulate without transfers and other means of redistribution - we consider this condition as a realistic one, since provision of public goods is one of the means of redistribution and there is hardly a substantial group of people who would be able to accumulate capital (or simply exist for a long period of time) without any of the public goods.

evidence supporting the existence of the Kuznets curve, noting the fact that the relation between growth and inequality is mixed: poor countries with high inequality exhibit lower growth, whereas rich countries have a positive relation between growth and inequality. This would mean that there exists a certain threshold, after which the effect turns into an opposite direction. We have to note that the data on regional Gini coefficients for Russia is available only for a limited number of years and, as stated in the Introduction, we specifically analyze economic growth and income distribution without an intention to empirically analyze them jointly. For the goals of our work a theoretical link between economic growth and income distribution is sufficient.

Proposition 18. *The relation between economic growth and income distribution is complex and non-linear; however, theoretical findings suggest that inequality decreases growth, rather than fosters it (with an exception to economic transitions).*

Bearing in mind the capital accumulation cases and developmental scenarios, Acemoglu and Robinson (2002, p. 195) formulate the theoretical revolution constraint:

$$\frac{h_t^r}{h_t^p} \leq \frac{\lambda(1-\mu_{remain})}{\mu_{remain}(1-\lambda)} = R_1 \tag{27}$$

Where the $1-\mu_{remain}$ is the fraction of wealth which would be destroyed after the revolution (the cost of a revolution), whereas μ_{remain} is the fraction of wealth which would remain. If the relation R_1 holds there will be no revolution. In equation (28) the notation is changed.

From equation (27) it follows that the probability of reaching the constraint depends on capital inequality between the rich and the poor, respected shares of the population and the costs of a revolution.

So far the revolution constraint involved human capital accumulation of the rich and the poor. This should not always be the case and one can formulate a revolution constraint solely based on income inequality. In Acemoglu and Robinson (2006, pp. 104-105) the revolution constraint is given a more intuitive form with the help of payoff functions:

$$y_p < \frac{\overline{y}(1-\mu_{cost})}{(1-\delta)} = R_2 \tag{28}$$

Where the left hand side is the fraction of the income, which would remain after the revolution (the authors reversed the notation in that case, by indicating that $1-\mu_{cost}$ is the remaining fraction after the revolution whereas the μ_{cost} is the cost of the revolution) divided by the share of the poor population, $1-\delta$. In this case, if the relation holds, a revolution will occur. We will denote this revolution constraint as R_2.

Proposition 19. *Related literature suggests that the revolution constraint can be formulated as function of income inequality.*

Recalling the relation of income growth to income inequality, Acemoglu and Robinson (2002) provide three consequent scenarios, lacking the graphical illustration. We will try to fill this gap with a very trivial numerical simulation using a parabolic function and growth and decay functions. The values were selected arbitrarily and serve only illustrative purposes.

First case is the Kuznets curve as in Acemoglu and Robinson (2002, p. 196), which has a concave shape, consistent with Kuznets (1955); however, having a completely different background. The revolution constraint is marked with a dashed horizontal line.

Fig. 13. Kuznets curve scenario

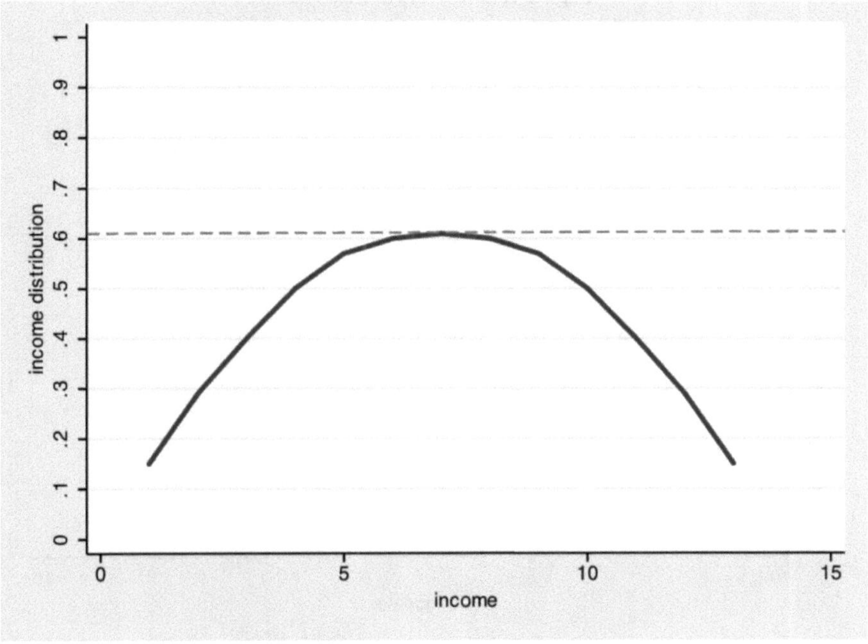

Source: proprietary simulation

Let us assume that the rich accumulate and the poor do not: the accumulation of income by the rich will generate increasing income inequality which would inevitably reach the threshold (the revolution constraint). As in Acemoglu and Robinson (2002, p. 196) after reaching the threshold, the rich would extend the franchise allowing the poor to accumulate capital, which would consequently lead to income convergence and decrease of inequality. One should note that for a such scenario the MVT is essential. However, democratization may not necessarily lead to a decrease in inequality: Remington (2011) notes that most democratic regions in Russia had relatively high levels of inequality. Therefore, additional conditions may apply.

In case of an autocratic disaster as in Acemoglu and Robinson (2002, p. 196), only the rich accumulate, or the poor accumulate in extremely small amounts compared to the accumulation of the rich. Even crossing the threshold does not change the income inequality. In our numeric simulation we assume a logistic function, since there would be a natural limit of the growth of income of the rich part of the society, othwerise the poor would face extinction. For this scenario the MVT is not relevant.

Fig. 14. Autocratic disaster

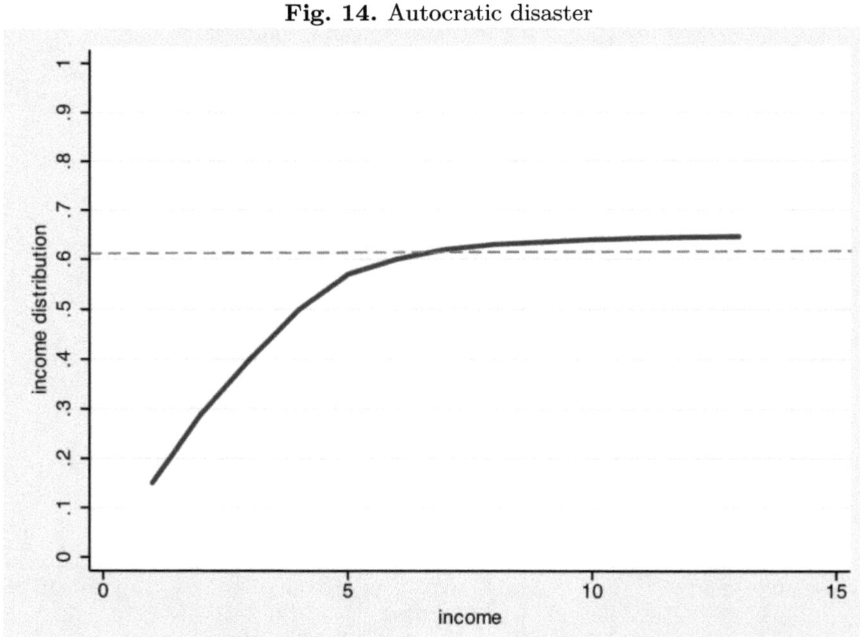

Source: proprietary simulation

The above-mentioned scenario arises an important question: in which cases the revolution constraint is binding? In case of an autocratic disaster, as in Acemoglu and Robinson (2002), an extremely low payoff after the revolution would make the poor ignore the revolution constraint. At a glance we can see that the revolution constraint may be missing important variables, such as different institutional proxies or variables for democracy or repressions. In addition, in Acemoglu and Robinson (2002) model possesses several drawbacks: the existence of the informal sector is acknowledged; however, the role of informal income is not analyzed; the capital accumulation process is presented in a dynamic way; however, the revolution constraint is clearly an attribute of comparative statics. Once considering the informal sector, we must include informal income and informal distribution in our equations - this would completely change the picture of an autocratic disaster, since the poor may be literally bribed with a share of the informal output to ignore the revolution constraint and the franchise may be extended in an informal way. Obviously the presence of a large informal sector would provide additional flexibility for the autocratic regime and the related elite.

Last case, described in Acemoglu and Robinson (2002, p. 197), is the East Asian miracle. This case is denoted by almost equally shared growing income with a starting point of relatively high income inequality. Due to certain institutional features, both the poor and the rich would accumulate with almost equal rates. In this case the revolution constraint is never met, thus revolution, democratization or franchise extension is not a necessary condition for income convergence. Acemoglu and Robinson (2002) relate this case to the examples of Taiwan and South Korea; however, with a lack of detail on the institutions, responsible for such convergence. Potentially, one could associate this scenario with informal institutions or traditions, adopted by the given society. Needless to say, this scenario is preferable.

Proposition 20. *From the above-mentioned literature three theoretical scenarios of income growth and income incequality can be formulated: the MVT-based political Kuznets curve, the autocratic disaster and the East Asian Miracle.*

Having considered the theoretical aspects of the political Kuznets curve and the related scenarios, we can now proceed to the stylized facts on Russia in order to apply the given theory. We will be particularly interested to find out which scenarios can be applied to Russia and whether a revolution constraint and income inequality play a role in the recent political developments in the regions.

Fig. 15. East Asian Miracle

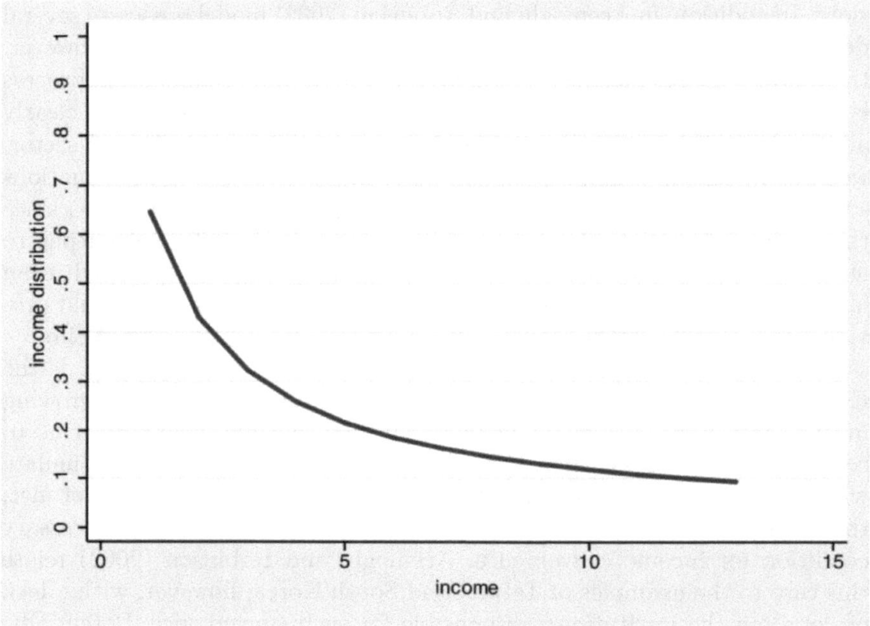

Source: proprietary simulation

3.2 Stylized facts on growth and distribution in Russia

The empirical observations on income inequality in the Russian regions deserve specific attention. These facts will guide us to the section of empirical estimation of the role of income inequality in predicting the probability of the recent protests in 2011-2012. In addition, we will try to explain the recent trends and link them to theoretical and empirical findings of other researchers.

One of the first facts to know is that according to Remington (2011, pp. 26-27), in Russia, wages tended to significantly lag behind prices. A large number of state enterprises were strangled in an economic stagnation during the transition period because of rapid changes in the ownership structure in the aftermath of the privatization in 1992 and due to inability to successfully compete with foreign producers, who gained access to the domestic market via imports. As in Remington (2011, pp. 40-47), large Russian state-owned companies often played a role of city-forming enterprises, having a certain burden of social responsibility. Thus during the first years of transition many workers, who were not fired, have faced a decline in the real wages due to rocketing prices. For example, in 1993 the CPI inflation in Russia was 874.6%, the following 1994 year ended with 307.6% inflation, decreasing in the subsequent periods[27] . Obviously, during such hyperinflation it is extremely complicated to adjust wages and moreover, redistribution payments, such as pensions or benefits. Remington (2011, p. 26) notes that lagging wages have been a relatively persistent problem, even after the first years of transformation. Another interesting aspect is the informal background of the wage distribution: Clarke (2002, p. 636) notes that the returns to education or experience are low in Russia and that "wage inequalities within industries are greater" than the ones "between industries". In addition, he emphasized a high wage inequality on the firm level. The wage differentiation can not be solely attributed to human capital theory, since a large number of informal institutions may distort the relationship of the returns to education and thus cause substantial disparities in wage distribution. Such differentiation can be also partly explained by the weakness of the Russian labour unions as in Remington (2011, p. 70).

A diminution of labour, which had quickly followed the first reforms, resulted in a large number of workers entering the unemployment pool who had a choice of receiving unemployment benefits during the job search or engage themselves with the shadow economy, which according to Kar and Freitas (2013, p. 12) on average during 1999-2007 was around 43.8% of the GDP. It is important to note that even in Acemoglu and Robinson (2002) the authors assume that production takes place in the formal sector. In the case of Russia, it appears that around 43.8% of the domestic product relates to the informal sector - thus enormous amount of funds is not taxed and does not enter the redistribution sphere. The presence of a large informal sector distorts the MVT elements of the political Kuznets curve: informal sector has an impact on the whole chain of redistribution starting with tax collection and ending with state expenditures, for example, on public goods. Once we account for the informal sector by including it in the revolution constraint, it will only depend on the share of the average output and the number of the poor, but also on the share of the average informal sector output. This would require a new set of conditions to make the constraint binding. Needless to say, the basic idea of the MVT theorem would be violated, unless competing political groups would be defining both formal and informal redistribution. This is extremely important, since this could partly explain the viability of the autocratic disaster: the Gini coefficient on the formal income distribution would be high; however, considering the informal sector and assuming a high incidence of corruption, the official income distribution may be very different from the distribution of the informal income, making the revolution constraint, based on official income inequality, irrelevant.

[27] Source: Goskomstat

Since we have mentioned the problem of indexation of the redistribution benefits, one should also mention the pension dynamics. It is wrong to assume that the value of a pension only has an impact on economic decisions of one layer of society, the pension recipients. People employed would discount their pensions since they would see this as a part of their future income. In addition, the younger generation may also consider pensions in their decision-making, regarding for example, education. According to Remington (2011, p. 69) the median regional pension in Russia during 2000-2006 was lower than the median subsistence level and was less than half the median wage - a striking fact. Even though the pension was indexed during these years, it had been lower than the median subsistence level. Of course, some regions enjoyed higher pension levels, for example Moscow, where pensions were partly subsidized by the city government. Nevertheless, an abnormally low level of redistribution benefits has been an issue for Russia for a relatively long period of time, and even the substantial increase in pensions after 2009 did not significantly change the picture.

Another fact which is worth our attention is that in Russia by the beginning of 2013 18.9% of families could be attributed to the middle class. This information alone is not valuable; however, around 20% of the Russia middle class are civil servants, policemen or security forces and other state-employed people[28]. In 2011 the total number of total civil servants has reached 1.6 million which has almost doubled since the beginning of the transition period[29]. Needless to say, most of the civil servants are members of the United Russia, the dominant centrist political party. Such composition of the middle class, part of which is obliged to display political loyalty, may significantly distort the MVT, because the voting outcome for a large fraction of the middle class would be already relatively easy to predict. The MVT can also be distorted by the elements of the institutional matrix, e.g. patrimonialism, as in Hedlund (2005). Bearing in mind the special structure of the middle class in Russia and the large informal sector we may question the validity of the MVT for Russia:

Proposition 21. *In Russia the MVT may be distorted by a large informal sector, a specific structure of the middle class and institutions. Therefore, the likelihood of the existence of a political Kuznets curve is small.*

Let us briefly summarize the given stylized facts on Russia: due to lagging and abnormally differentiated wages, a large informal sector of the economy reaching up to 43.8% of the GDP, which distorts tax collection and redistribution, including provision of public goods and due to relatively low redistribution benefits, income inequality in Russia is inevitably rising.

[28] Source: http://lenta.ru/news/2013/04/04/middle/

[29] Source: Goskomstat

Let us try to display the Kuznets curve in time for Russia. We will use a quadratic fit, which would reveal the concave curvature, providing it exists.

As we see on Figure 16, the trend is linear and there is no curvature and thus, the Kuznets curve scenario can not be validated during this time period. In fact, the empirical observations point at the autocratic disaster if we recall Figure 14, or at the left half of the Kuznets curve, as in Figure 13; however, what if we consider a spatial version of the Kuznets curve and try to make a snapshot for Russian regions for a given year? Applying a quadratic fit in this case yields interesting results. With Moscow city having the highest Gini coefficient of 0.505, the curve reaches its peak (see Figure 17). Tyumen, Sakhalin and Chukotskaya oblast add the curvature: extremely rich regions with a low population density have higher GRP values and enjoy a relatively lower income inequality. We should highlight the fact that in the spatial dimension one could speculate on the existence of a concave relation between income and income inequality; however, if we exclude the Tyumen, the Sakhalin and the Chukotskaya oblast, the fit would be linear for the remaining regions.

Fig. 16. Income inequality and income: Russia (1995-2010)

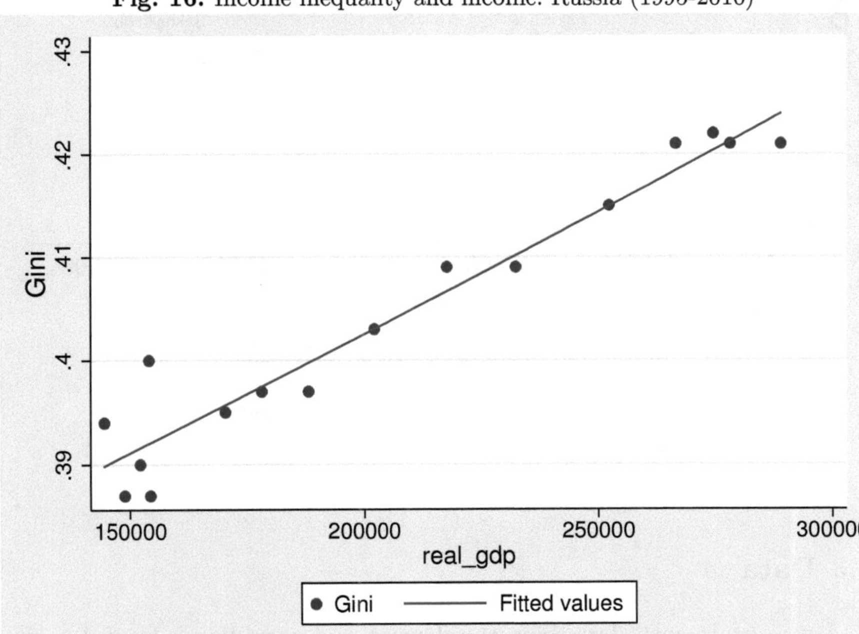

Data: Goskomstat, aggregated real GDP per capita

Another fact on income is a very weak catching up to Moscow - this fact has been mentioned in Chapter 1, proposition 5. Most of the regions are following Moscow at the distance of around 0.5 of the Moscow's GRP per capita. This creates sharp contrasts and persistent disparities among regions. Therefore it is hard to assign a developmental scenario for Russia. Operating with the terms as in Acemoglu and Robinson (2002, p. 196), we could speculate that Russia is on the left half of the political Kuznets curve and moving towards a constraint, or simply experiences an autocratic disaster.

Fig. 17. Spatial Kuznets curve for the Russian regions (2010)

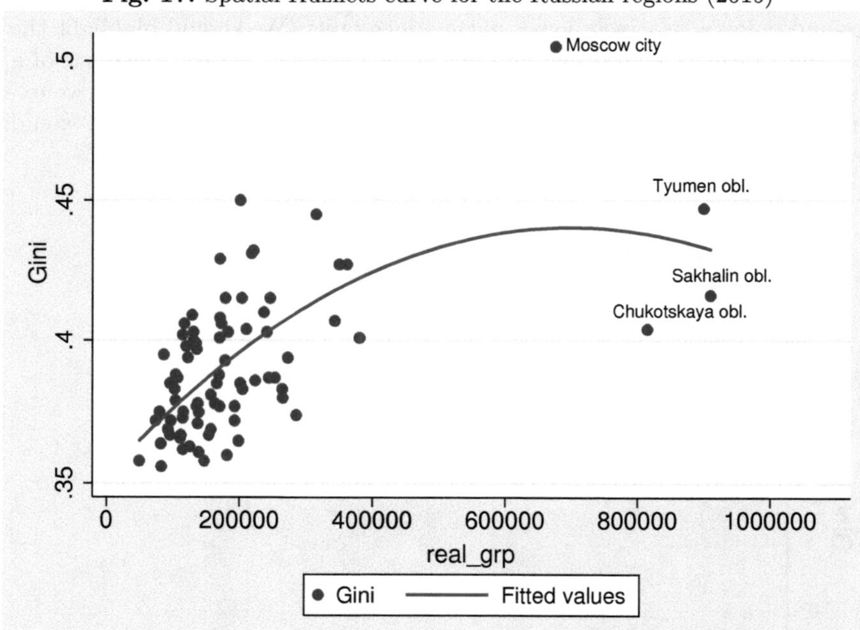

Data: Goskomstat, real GRP per capita

3.3 Data

Let us start with describing the dataset and providing a brief description of the variables involved in Table 10. In order to correctly interpret the estimation one should first consider the nature of the data. The seletion of the regions resembles the list in Chapter 1; however, the data on governor's family income for the Karelia republic and the Murmansk oblast was not available. Regarding the description of the variables, most of which have an intuitive interpretation, one should focus on several details in order to understand the coefficients obtained in Table 11. Firstly, the variable "protest" takes a binary form of 1 (for multiple protests in the regional capital and at least one other location with strictly more than 300 participants reported by official sources) or 0 (if otherwise). This benchmark definition is introduced to minimize the number of false or exaggerated reports and cut off spontaneous events with no political purpose.

Table 10. Data for the logistic regression

Variable	Obs	Mean	Std. Dev.	Min	Max	Description
protest	79	0.3375	0.4758404	0	1	1 if protest in regions with with >300 people and 0 otherwise
gov_income	77	50800	282000	900	2270000	income of the governor's family in in thousands of roubles, 2010
ln_gov_income	77	15.52832	1.249073	13.71015	21.54234	logarithm of the income of the governeour's family, 2011
gini_100	79	39.18481	2.56561	35.6	50.5	Gini coefficient*100
avg_income	79	393	144	186	1057	Average annual family income, 2010, thousands of roubles
ln(gov_income/ agv_income)	77	2.7024	1.248641	1.237599	8.725481	ratio
democ	79	29.0126	6.28489	17	45	Carnegie Center democracy index for Russian regions, 2000-2004
crisis_100	79	4.17484	11.66174	-29.45185	30.74398	real GRP change after the crisis in 2008*100
ln_distmsc	79	7.065677	1.505416	0	9.382275	spatial distance from Moscow, logarithm of kilometres

Data: Goskomstat, Carnegie Center, Vedomosti.ru, news networks, Abramov (1965)

The information obtained from the federal and regional news[30] suggests that the protests, as identified in terms of our approach, during 2011-2012 took place in: the Ivanovo oblast, the Moskovskaya oblast, the Tulskaya oblast, Moscow city, the Arkhangelskaya oblast, the Vologodskaya oblast, the Kaliningradskaya oblast, the Pskovskaya oblast, Saint-Petersburg, the Krasnodarskaya oblast, the Astrakhanskaya oblast, the Volgogradskaya oblast, the Rostovskaya oblast, the Bashkortastan, the Tatarstan, the Udmurt republics, the Permskiy krai, the Nizhegorodskaya oblast, the Samarskaya oblast, the Sverdlovskaya oblast, the Tyumen oblast, the Chelyabinskaya oblast, the Altaiskiy krai, the Irkutskaya oblast, the Novosibirskaya oblast, the Tomskaya oblast, the Primorskaya oblast. In fact 33.75% of the regions were to a certain extent involved in protests. Secondly, one should note that the income of the regional governeors is derived

[30] Inluding but not limited to RBC, INTERFAX, RIA

from the tax declarations (available on the websites of regional administrations) and from the Vedomosti.ru database. This value represents the total nominal family income of the governor, namely the income of the governor and his wife, for cases when the governor may be able to outmanoeuvre the prohibition business activities for civil servants and delegate such activities to their closest relatives. In Chapter 2 we have briefly mentioned one of the consequences of the resource curse: the rent-seeking behavour. Regional governors are perfect examples of it, keeping in mind that since 2005-2011 the governors were assigned and not elected. Libman et al. (2012, p. 529) has compared Russian governors with "roving bandits". In our models, we also use the relation of the governor's family income to average family income as a proxy for income inequality and the already mentioned social "impatience" or tension: a Gini coefficient is a distant macroeconomic measure published post factum and with a substantial delay, whereas the governor's income is publically available once the related tax declaration is submitted and thus the poor can be informed about the income of the rich. Moreover, the submission deadline of tax declaration is usually on the 1st of April for the last calendar year, e.g. the 1st April 2011 for the calendar year 2010, which makes it a reasonable variable for predicting the protests of 2011-2012. The variable "democ" represents the impact of civil liberties and political rights on predicting the probability of the protests. Another interesting variable is "crisis", which captures the impact of the recent global financial crisis on the protests: here we take the first growth rate of the real GRP per capita after 2008, when the crisis started. Disance to Moscow is added to investigate the role of the spatial factor. Variables "gini" and "crisis" are multiplied by 100 to simplify the calculation of the marginal effects. The marginal effects are calculated as in Wooldridge (2002, pp. 465-470) at means. It is crucial to note that marginal effects of variables which were transformed into logarithms would represent elasticities, in other words, for such variables $\partial y/\partial x$ would represent the percentage change in the probability if the explanatory variable changes by 1%. For other variables $\partial y/\partial x$ denotes marginal effect on the probability after a change in the explanatory variable by 1 point.

3.4 Empirical strategy, analysis of protests and results

Having discovered sharp income and output disparities and main reasons for growing income inequality in Russia, we now have to proceed in our analysis and investigate whether income inequality is responsible for the recent protests during 2011-2012.

At first glance at the map, which displays the distribution of Gini coefficient and protests in a binary form, one can notice that in most cases

Fig. 18. Income distribution (2010) and protests (2011-2012)

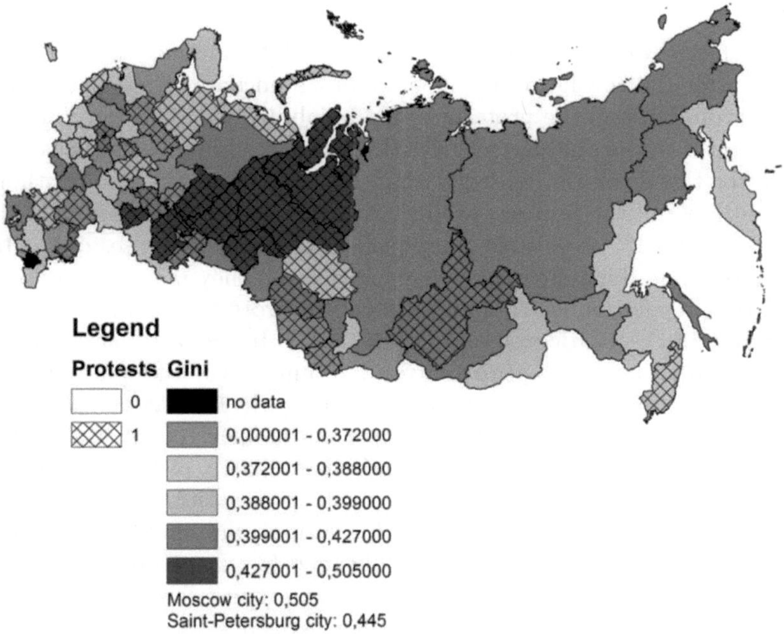

Data: Goskomstat and news networks

the protests tend to arise in the regions where income inequality is relatively high; however, this conclusion is highly speculative without robust empirical proof. In order to investigate the impact of the income inequality on the probability of protests, we applied a latent variable approach as in Wooldridge (2002, Chpt. 15 and p. 458) and a logit regression based on three models to ensure the robustness of our results. Last model has two specifications: with outliers and without. In addition, we will control for the effects of democracy, economic depression and the spatial factor. The latter would help us to check if the protests were centralized. From the map it follows that a certain clustering effect of the protests was observed.

The empirical approach which was selected to analyze the role of income inequalities in determining the probabilty of protests, is derived from the latent variable framework, as in Wooldridge (2002, pp. 458-459). Let us assume that there is a latent variable ϑ denoting achievement of the constraint, if we recall the second revolution constraint in the equation (28) from Acemoglu and Robinson (2006, pp. 104-105):

$$\vartheta = \frac{\overline{y}(1 - \mu_{cost})}{(1 - \delta)} - y_p \tag{29}$$

Then if this variable ϑ is positive, it would mean that the payoff of the poor after the revolution is higher than the income of the poor without the revolution and the protests would be observable. Therefore, in this case the constraint is binding, whereas if the latent variable is negative, the payoff after the revolution is lower than the income of the poor without the revolution and the protests would not occur. The protests are only the "tip of the iceberg", observable consequences of latent processes of capital accumulation and dynamic income inequalities and they may not necessarily lead to a revolution. A similar approach to protests was mentioned in Manukyan (2011), and Bozzoli and Brück (2011). In the latter case the authors used a multinomial logit to analyse determinants of different grades of participation in the protests in the Ukraine. Empirical works on the recent protests in Russia are scarce - for example, in Sobolev (2012), the author uses the quantitative dependent variable. Sobolev (2012, p. 17) uses the opposition reports and the police data to construct an arithmetic average of the number of protesters. Nevertheless this variable automatically includes a measurement error: the opposition would tend to exaggerate the number of protesters, whereas the police would tend to report lower numbers. In addition, in Sobolev (2012), the political Kuznets curve is not considered a theoretical ground of the empirical modeling: income inequality is included in only one of the models and turns to be insignificant in explaining the number of protesters. We implement a simple binary dependent variable in order to minimize such empirical issues. Nevertheless, we admit risks of measurement errors.

We have to make one more note: the protests, which took place in Russia during 2011-2012, were the effect or the manifestation of a certain problem. It is of paramount importance to examine this cause empirically. We disregard spurious protests of unclear nature or mass events like "flash mobs". As in Sobolev (2012, p. 21), one of the causes was the parliament election results. We focus on deep economic determinants, such as income inequality and the impact of growth or stagnation after the crisis. Thus, we see the protests as an effect driven by an economic cause. Nevertheless, we leave room for institutional and spatial variables in our models.

The first logistic model is designed in order to verify the role of income inequalities in determining the probability of protests:

$$protest_i = \beta_0 + \beta_1 gini\_100_i + u_i \tag{30}$$

Where $protest_i$ is a binary variable, $gini\_100_i$ is the Gini coefficient multiplied by 100, βs are coefficients and u_i is the error. If we recall equation (29), the latent variable description, we would expect to discover that that higher income inequality corresponds to a higher probability of protests. Thus, the next proposition could be formulated in the following way:

Fig. 19. Bivariate prediction of protests based in income inequality

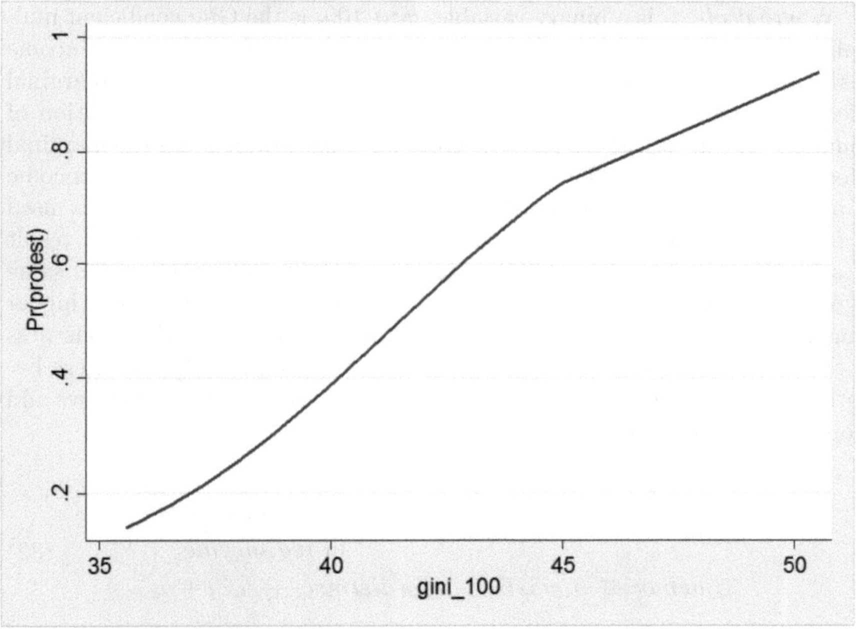

Data: Goskomstat

Proposition 22. *A risk of protests positively depends on the income inequality; therefore a revolution constraint based on income inequality may be empirically valid.*

The estimates from model (30) are presented in Table 11. Gini coefficient from 2010 turns out to be a significant predictor of protests during 2011-2012 in a bi-variate model. The marginal effect of a one point increase of the Gini-index would results in a 6.76% increase in the probability of protests. The positive relation between the protest risk and income inequality is displayed on Figure 19. Proposition 22 was partly proven in the bivariate framework: the coefficient on income inequality was significant. Let us now verify the robustness of our results and add another inequality proxy: the governor's family income.

Proposition 23. *The governor's family income is a better income inequality proxy due to its public availability. A more advanced proxy for the income*

inequality is the governor's family income and the ratio of it to the average family income - this variable will be used in the extended models.

$$protest_i = \beta_0 + \beta_1 gini\_100_i + \beta_2 \ln gov\_income_i + u_i \qquad (31)$$

Where $protest_i$ is a binary variable, $gini\_100_i$ is the Gini coefficient multiplied by 100, $\ln gov\_income_i$ is the logarithm of the family annual income of the regional governor, βs are coefficients and u_i is the error. The marginal effects presented in Table 11 are of extreme importance. In estimation of equation (31) the significance of the Gini index has lowered and the marginal effect dropped to 6.3%. The marginal effect of the governor's family income is in fact presented as an elasticity coefficient since the variable is used in logarithms: a 1% increase in the governor's family income would result in a 16.75% rise in the probability of protests. This effect is on the same significance level as the Gini index, but has an almost three times higher magnitude. Let us postulate further propositions and check the robustness of the latter income inequality proxy. In order to empirically test these hypotheses and ensure the robustness of our income inequality proxies, we add more variables to the model:

$$\begin{aligned} protest_i = \beta_0 + \beta_1 gini\_100_i + \beta_2 \frac{\ln gov\_income_i}{\ln avg\_income_i} + \\ \beta_3 democ_i + \beta_4 crisis_i + \beta_5 \ln distmsc_i + \beta_6 Z_i + u_i \end{aligned} \qquad (32)$$

Where $protest_i$ is a binary variable, $gini\_100_i$ is the Gini coefficient by 100, $\ln gov\_income_i$ is the family annual income of the regional governor, $\ln avg\_income_i$ is the average family income, $democ_i$ is the Carnegie Center democracy index, $crisis_i$ is the change of the GRP per capita after the crisis of 2008, $\ln distmsc_i$ is the logarithm of the distance from Moscow, Z_i are additional controls, e.g., share of urban population in the region, βs are coefficients and u_i is the error.

Specification (32.1) includes outliers and in (32.2) we have excluded Arkhangelsk oblast, Krasnodar krai and Krasnoyarsk krai - these regions had the highest leverage after (32.1). Results obtained for model (32) and presented in Table 11 require additional explanations. Firstly, the Gini index loses any statistical significance, which now corresponds to the results in Sobolev (2012). Even though the results for the Gini index are not robust, one should not conclude that income inequality does not play a role as a determinant of protests: effect of the governor's family income is significantly higher in the expanded model. The ratio of income of the elite to the average income allows us to additionally control for the average income in the region. Specification (32.1) suggests that a 1% increase in the ratio of the family annual income of the regional governor to the average family income would result in a rise of the risk of protests by 23.18% - the effect is now significant on all conventional levels, even after including proxies for democracy, economic depression and the spatial factor. After removing the outliers in (32.2) this effect became less significant and increased to 26.82%. Removing the outliers improved the fit of the model as can be seen from the Likelihood ratio test and from the ratios as well.

The effect of democracy in (32.1) is modest; however, sufficient to support proposition 24: a 1 point change in the democracy index would increase the probability of protests by 3.55%. Without the outliers in (32.2) this effect is less significant is constitutes 3.51%. One may assume that the Carnegie center democracy index captures political activity of the population: this would be a logical explanation of the discovered effect.

Proposition 24. *The degree of democratization has a positive impact on the protest probability.*

The impact of the crisis is highly significant in (32.1) and (32.2): a rise in the GRP per capita after the crisis in 2008 by 1% would lower the risk of protests by 3.16%, whereas the drop by 1% would have an opposite effect and would increase the risk by 3.16%. Consequently, in (32.2) the magnitude of this effect is 2.84%.

Proposition 25. *The magnitude of the economic depression after 2008 has a positive impact on the protest probability (the deeper the economic downturn after the crisis in 2008 was, the higher is the risk of protests). Therefore economic growth or downturn may have an impact on the risk of protests.*

This evidence supports proposition 25 and hints at the deep economic nature of the protests. Since the GRP dynamics would highly correlate with unemployment we do not include the latter in our model and use GRP per capita as a proxy for economic activity. We can support proposition 26: the results from Table 11 coincide with the visualization of the protest distribution on the map. The distribution of the protests was not centralized, but rather dispersed. Nevertheless from the Figure 18 alone we can conclude that the neighboring regions had a greater chance of transmitting protests: spatial distribution of protests hints on a certain clustering effect.

Proposition 26. *The protests are not centralized, but rather clustered.*

Table 11. Logit estimates of protest determinants (with Marginal Effects)

VARIABLES	(30) Protest	$\partial y/\partial x$ ME	(31) Protest	$\partial y/\partial x$ ME	(32.1) Protest	$\partial y/\partial x$ ME	(32.2) Protest	$\partial y/\partial x$ ME
gini_100	0.306***	0.06768***	0.285**	0.06311**	0.0918	0.016999	0.0787	0.00613
	(0.112)	(0.02493)	(0.117)	(0.0259)	(0.163)	(0.03056)	(0.253)	(0.02045)
	2.726	2.72	2.429	2.44	0.564	0.56	0.31	0.3
ln_gov_income			0.755**	0.1675312**				
			(0.305)	(0.06937)				
			2.477	2.41				
ln(gov_income/ agv_income)					1.253***	0.2318847***	3.444***	0.26826*
					(0.443)	(0.08601)	(1.193)	(0.14477)
					2.827	2.7	2.887	1.85
democ					0.192**	0.0355**	0.451**	0.0351*
					(0.0859)	(0.01602)	(0.201)	(0.01834)
					2.232	2.22	2.236	1.91
crisis_100					-0.171***	-0.0316***	-0.365***	-0.0284**
					(0.0508)	(0.00897)	(0.117)	(0.01409)
					-3.363	-3.53	-3.108	-2.02
ln_distmsc					0.158	0.0292	0.669	0.05209
					(0.285)	(0.0529)	(0.432)	(0.038)
					0.555	0.55	1.548	1.37
Constant	-12.69***		-23.59***		-14.10**		-36.29**	
	(4.428)		(6.519)		(6.858)		(15.01)	
	-2.865		-3.618		-2.056		-2.418	
Pseudo R2	0.0904		0.1875		0.4816		0.7396	
Likelihood ratio	9.18		18.24		48.05		70.01	
Observations	79		77		77		74	
Outliers					Included		Excluded	
Control for urban population					x		x	
Likelihood ratio test (32.1) vs (32.2)							0	

Standard errors in parentheses
*** p<0.01, ** p<0.05, * p<0.1
Source: proprietary estimation

3.5 Summary of Chapter 3

Considering the MVT to be an integral element of the political Kuznets curve, a concave relation between income and income inequality driven by political factors, we pointed out several issues related to the validity of the MVT in Russia. The three scenarios, presented in Acemoglu and Robinson (2002), the political Kuznets curve (MVT based), the autocratic disaster (for which the MVT is irrelevant) and the Asian wonder, help us to classify the situation in Russia as a left half of the Kuznets curve or, what seems more disturbing, the autocratic disaster. In the case of the political Kuznets curve, the rise of income would correspond to the rise of income inequality until a certain constraint would be met, as in Figure 13. In case when the constraint is met, the society would undergo transformation of a structural and political nature, which would lead to a more efficient taxation and redistribution resulting in a decrease in income inequality. Regarding Russia, Figure 16 clearly suggests a monotonic positive linear relationship between income and income inequality. Nevertheless, we were able to construct a spatial Kuznets curve for the Russian regions for the year 2010, as in Figure 17. Having found mixed evidence of the Kuznets curve, we investigated the validity of its political aspect - the revolution constraint. In order to analyze the empirical relation of the recent protests in Russia during 2011-2012 to income inequality proxies, we applied the latent variable framework and a set of logistic models. This approach was selected in order to at least partly outmaneuver the measurement error, a potential issue of protest movement measurement as in Sobolev (2012).

We found that income inequality proxies such as the Gini index, the governor's family income and the ratio of the governor's family income to average family income are significant positive determinants of the risk of the protests. The latter variable turned out to be extremely robust, even after controlling for democracy index, the 2008 crisis consequences and the spatial factor. In model (30) estimations, a 1 point marginal increase in the Gini index would result in a 6.76% increase in the probability of protests. In the extended model (32.1) and (32.2) as in Table 11, the estimates suggest that a 1% increase in the ratio of the governor's family income to average family income in the region would on average increase the risk of protests by 23.18% or by 26.82% without the outliers. We found that the effect of democracy on the probability of protests is also significant: a rise of the democracy index by 1 point would increase the probability of protests by around 3.5% in specifications (32.1) and (32.2). The economic crisis of 2008 also contributed to the development of protests: a drop in GRP per capita after 2008 by 1% would increase the risk of protests by 3.16% or by 2.84% without the outliers in (32.2). We could not find any evidence of protest centralization since the variable "distance from Moscow" was not significant. However, the visualization of spatial distribution of protests allows us to report a certain clustering effect, since mostly neighboring regions had experienced protests.

4

Conclusion

Empirical analysis of the economic growth and income distribution was performed in several steps and each chapter has a separate conclusion summary. In Chapter 1 we analysed growth determinants and convergence in a cross-section and dynamic frameworks. Chapter 2 focused on one of the main threats to economic growth in Russia: the resource curse and its impact on the human capital, which was noted to be a robust determinant of growth in Chapter 1. In Chapter 3 we proceed to the core topic of the research: economic growth and income distribution. Referring to the political Kuznets curve, we conduct an empirical analysis of the recent protests in Russia and show that income inequality as well as economic growth (and downturn) after the crisis are robust determinants of the risk of protests. Below we summarize the findings and conclusions for each chapter and suggest our policy recommendations.

In Chapter 1 we introduced the theoretical framework and the neoclassical Solow growth model demonstrating its key features with the help of a numerical simulation. After examining the extensions of this model, we proceeded to literature overview on empirics of growth and our own analysis of growth determinants with the help of cross-section OLS growth regressions and dynamic panel data system GMM estimation. Prior to the estimations, we graphically demonstrated the presence of β-convergence and the absence of σ-convergence for the time period of 1995-2010. The main empirical findings from the OLS growth regressions for 1995-2007 were the following: the annual speed of unconditional cross-section β-convergence was around 1.895% from specification (12.1), to the highest estimate of the annual speed of conditional cross-section convergence 3.898% from specification (12.5); fragile positive impact of real investments per capita was detected around 1.534% from specification (12.2); fragile negative impact of the share of civil servants in the employed population of -1.057% of growth from specification (12.4); robust positive impact of the share of the employed population with higher education of 0.136% from specification (12.4) and 0.12% from the extended specification (12.7); fragile negative impact of the Carnegie Center democracy index of -0.124%[31] from the extended specification (12.6) excluding outliers; robust negative decrease in growth by 0.370 for each additional 1000 kilometers distance from Moscow form the extended specification (12.7) with treated outliers. Regions with largest cities (Moscow, Saint-Petersburg, Novosibirsk, Sverdlovsk, Nizhniy Novgorod) tended to grow faster; however, this effect was not significant. The cross-section regressions were performed with outliers, without outliers, and with weighted outliers. Highlighting the problem of "too many instruments" in the two-step system GMM estimation for 2000-2007, we reported the related results together with autocorrelation tests, Sargan and Hansen tests and white noise test on residuals. The results suggest than in the dynamic framework real investments per capita are a significant positive determinants of growth and the speed of dynamic convergence ranges from 1.13% to 2.98% from specifications (13.2 and 13.3), including 5.5% from the previous work of the author, Kufenko (2012, p. 12). The system GMM results should be taken into account with caution due to 45-48 instruments against 328 observations used, even though all the tests were passed. In order to ensure transparency and quality of our results, endogenous and exogenous instruments are listed in the model specifications and tests statistics are reported in the Appendix.

Chapter 2 focused on the resource curse, bearing in mind that we consider it to be one the main problems to the economic growth in Russia. Referring to Chapter 1, we established the fact that oil and gas extraction per capita did not have a significant coefficient. We acknowledged the fact the the resource curse and its impact on the economy requires a more detailed investigation and theoretical modelling, since in some cases we simply lack the data. We examined the sectoral and sub-sectoral change in the Russian economy since 2005 and found that the proportions of extraction to manufacturing are relatively constant; however, we detected a sub-sectoral shift: since 2005 the share of fuels in manufacturing has increased from 16 to 19.9%. After the discussion of the economic and institutional interpretations of the resource curse including the Dutch disease, regulatory capture and rent-seeking behaviour, which are the dominant interpretations in the existing literature, we noted that historical path dependence is also important: the resource abundance may not necessarily promote the rent-seeking behaviour; however, if the rent-seeking behaviour is already historically integrated in the institutional matrix, the likelihood of a blessing with natural resources turning into a curse would increase. In addition, we argued that the

[31] As we have noted, this impact may be nonliniear.

demand for human capital under resource abundance may be lower as it is often mentioned in the literature. Afterwards, we examined the wage differentiation emphasizing that the wages in education in 2010 were around 0.67 of the average wage and establish a negative trend in researchers per million population in Russia overlaying it on cumulative migration. Acknowledging the brain-drain problem, due to the absence of empirical data, we applied game theory to model the decision-making of human capital bearers and the state. One of the main theoretical findings is that human capital bearers decide whether they stay in the domestic pool of researchers or switch by comparing their monetary and non-monetary (e.g. institutional) payoffs. The resource curse can be formulated as a set of conditions, under which the human capital bearer will most likely leave the domestic pool of researchers. A flow of related game outcomes will form and a certain belief will establish, which will lead to a vicious circle since this belief will impact on the decision-making process of the state regarding the investments in human capital. Thus, the resource curse poses a great threat to human capital and a potential threat to long-term growth in Russia.

The core topic of our research, economic growth and income distribution, is discussed in Chapter 3. Considering the political Kuznets curve, a concave relation between income and income inequality driven by political factors, we pointed out several issues related to the empirics in Russia. The three scenarios, derived from the related literature, the Kuznets curve, the autocratic disaster (for which the MVT is irrelevant) and the Asian wonder, help us to classify the situation in Russia as a left half of the Kuznets curve or the autocratic disaster. Regarding Russia, Figure 16 clearly suggests a monotonic positive linear relationship between income and income inequality. Nevertheless, in the spatial dimension we were able to find mixed evidence of a Kuznets curve. In order to analyze the empirical relation of the recent protests in Russia during 2011-2012 to income inequality proxies, we applied the latent variable framework and a set of logistic models. We found that income inequality proxies such as the Gini index and the governors family income and its relation to the average family income in the region, are significant positive determinants of the risk of the protests; however, only the latter two were robust whereas the Gini coefficient had a fragile effect, which vanished after adding the controls. In model (30) estimations, a 1 point marginal increase in the Gini index would result in a 6.76% increase in the probability of protests. In the extended model (32.1) and (32.2) as in Table 11, the estimates suggest that a 1% increase in the ratio of the governor's family income to average family income in the region would on average increase the risk of protests by 23.18% or by 26.82% without the outliers. The robustness of the latter effect and extremely high income levels of the families of regional governors may signal the presence of the historically established "kormlenie" phenomenon as in Hedlund (2005, p. 15) which was mentioned in Chapter 2 as an example of the rent-seeking behavior of regional authorities, who were entitled to literally "feed" from local population. Obviously, the population would be unhappy about such governors. We discovered that the effect of democracy on the probability of protests is also significant: a rise of the Carnegie Center (democracy index by 1 point would increase the probability of protests by around 3.5% in specifications (32.1) and (32.2). The economic crisis of 2008 also contributed to the development of protests: a drop in GRP per capita after 2008 by 1% would increase the risk of protests by 3.16% or by 2.84% without the outliers in (32.2). This effect confirms the fact that economic growth (or downturn) is of crucial importance in determining the risk of protests. The visualization of spatial distribution of protests on Figure 18 allows us to report a certain clustering effect, since mostly neighboring regions had experienced protests and Moscow could not be considered as a main center of protests.

Considering our propositions, we would like to suggest the following policy recommendations. Regarding proposition 4 and 5, high regional disparities and majority of regions following the output level of Moscow without significant signs of catching up, we recommend further investigations of the situation in the regions lagging behind and determining success factors for regions which are catching up.

We would like to issue a general recommendation on offsetting the diminishing returns to capital, which was partially inherited from the times of the Soviet Union: in order to offset or minimize this effect, we recommend policies on fostering innovations and adaptation of more efficient technologies. Subsidies and tax cuts on the use of more efficient machinery could be controlled and enforced by numerous conditions in order to encourage the use of more efficient technologies. Bearing in mind proposition 14 on lower demand for human capital under resource abundance, such policies could indirectly stimulate demand for human capital.

Considering proposition 9, since the increase in the distance from Moscow tends to lead to lower growth rates, we would encourage the state to develop infrastructure (or stimulate its development) for a more efficient communication with distant regions. Indeed, currently there is only one railway route linking the West and the East of Russia and transportation costs and risks are high, creating a serious bias for economic growth. This would require a thorough revision of the existing infrastructure and capacities inherited from the Soviet Union and the demand for additional routes under present conditions.

Referring to proposition 8, human capital is one of the most robust growth determinants in Russian regions; however, as we stated in proposition 13 and 14, there is an obvious diminution of human capital in Russia.

This can be attributed to a lowering demand for human capital: according to the game-theoretic outcome, the human capital bearer is determined to leave the domestic pool of researchers under the conditions simulating a resource curse as stated in proposition 16. A series of such outcomes would create a vicious circle and disrupt investments in human capital as in proposition 17. Thus, we recommend provision of larger research grants under stricter conditions, stimulation and motivation of researchers who have left Russia to return home and disseminate the obtained knowledge. For these purposes, as it was shown in Chapter 2, monetary stimulus is not sufficient - a more attractive institutional environment for researchers is necessary.

This allows us to proceed to the next recommendation. As we stated in proposition 15, rent-seeking behavior may be a serious issue. However, dealing with such indirect products of the resource curse such as corruption may be possible only under independent judiciary system. Considering proposition 23, we could recommend fully restoring regional elections[32] to avoid the problem of "roving bandits" as in Libman et al. (2012).

Propositions 22 and 23 on the significant role of income inequalities in determining the recent protests suggest revision and optimization of the redistribution schemes and taxation, urging for transparency of civil servants, governmental agencies and large state enterprises. In 2003, the "tax police" was abolished in Russia and its functions were partially distributed among different state agencies. Bearing in mind that almost half of the output in Russia is involved in the informal sector, as we mentioned in Chapter 3, such special entity could improve the situation. Although, it should not turn into an instrument of economic repressions.

All these recommendations would be inefficient if one does not take the institutional matrix into account: for example, the "tax police" could potentially become an instrument of repressions, and development of infrastructure may also fail because of corruption. This fact puts enforcement of the rule of law and property rights on the top of the list.

We would identify the following potential issues for future research: investigation of factors crucial for catching up among Russian regions; empirical analysis of the brain-drain problem; considering the Russian infrastructure from the point of view of the economic geography, and a more detailed analysis of the protests based on the old and additional data and a non-parametric analysis of economic growth and income inequality.

[32] In 2013 the elections were de jure restored; however, with a large number of conditions and restrictions making their results de facto vulnerable to manipulation from the side of the regional parliaments and other authorities.

References

Abramov, A. (1965). *The Manual of Tariffs N. 4, book 3, Tariff distances between key transport locations.* Moscow: Transport.

Abramovitz, M. (1986). Catching up, forging ahead, and falling behind. *The Journal of Economic History*, 46(2):385–406.

Acemoglu, D. (2009). *Introduction to Modern Economic Growth.* Princeton: Princeton Univeristy Press.

Acemoglu, D., Johnson, S., and Robinson, J. A. (2001). The colonial origins of comparative development: An empirical investigation. *The American Economic Review*, 91(5):1369–1401.

Acemoglu, D. and Robinson, J. (2002). The political economy of the kuznets curve. *Review of Development Economics*, 6(2):183–203.

Acemoglu, D. and Robinson, J. (2006). *Economic Origins of Dictatorship and Democracy.* New York: Cambridge University Press.

Achen, C. (2001). Why lagged dependent variables can suppress the explanatory power of other independent variables. Working Paper. Available at: http://www.princeton.edu/csdp/events/Achen121201/achen.pdf.

Aghion, P. and Howitt, P. (1997). *Endogenous Growth Theory.* MIT Press Books, The MIT Press.

Aghion, P. and Howitt, P. (2008). *The Economics of Growth.* Cambridge: MIT Press.

Albouy, D. Y. (2008). The Colonial Origins of Comparative Development: An Investigation of the Settler Mortality Data. WP N. 14130, NBER Working Papers.

Alesina, A. and Rodrik, D. (1994). Distributive politics and economic growth. *The Quarterly Journal of Economics*, 109(2):465–490.

Aoki, M. (2001). *Toward a Comparative Institutional Analysis*, volume 1 of *MIT Press Books.* The MIT Press.

Arellano, M. and Bond, S. (1991). Some tests of specification for panel data: Monte carlo evidence and an application to employment equations. *The Review of Economic Studies*, 58(2):277–297.

Arellano, M. and Bover, O. (1995). Another look at the instrumental variable estimation of error-components models. *Journal of Econometrics*, 68(1):29–51.

Arrow, K. J. (1962). The economic implications of learning by doing. *The Review of Economic Studies*, 29(3):155–173.

Auty, R. M. (1998). Resource abundance and economic development. Research Paper N. 44, United Nations University and World Institute for Development Economics Research.

Barro, R. J. (1991). Economic growth in a cross section of countries. *The Quarterly Journal of Economics*, 106(2):407–443.

Barro, R. J. (2000). Inequality and growth in a panel of countries. *Journal of Economic Growth*, 5(1):5–32.

Becker, G. S. (1975). *Human Capital: A Theoretical and Empirical Analysis, with Special Reference to Education, 2nd ed.* Number beck75-1 in NBER Books. National Bureau of Economic Research, Inc.

Belsley, D. A. (1987). Collinearity and least squares regression: Comment: Well-conditioned collinearity indices. *Statistical Science*, 2(1):86–91.

Berkowitz, D. and DeJong, D. (2003). Policy reform and growth in post-Soviet Russia. *European Economic Review*, 47(2):337–352.

Black, D. (1948). On the rationale of group decision-making. *Journal of Political Economy*, 56(1):23–34.

Blundell, R. and Bond, S. (1998). Initial conditions and moment restrictions in dynamic panel data models. *Journal of Econometrics*, 87(1):115–143.

Boix, C. and Svolik, M. (2007). Non-tyrannical autocracies. Available at: http://www.sscnet.ucla.edu/polisci/cpworkshop/papers/Boix.pdf.

Bolle, M. and Sahli, A. (2007). Autocracy, democracy and growth: Theoretical foundations. Paper Presented at the Conference "The Institutional and Social Dynamics of Growth and Redistribution", Lucca, 10-12 December. Available at: http://growth-institutions.ec.unipi.it/pages/Democracy/democracy.pdf.

Bond, S., Hoeffler, A., and Temple, J. (2001). GMM estimation of empirical growth models. Economics Papers 2001-W21, Economics Group, Nuffield College.

Bozzoli, C. and Brück, T. (2011). Determinants of protests: Longitudinal evidence from Ukraine's orange revolution. Discussion Papers of DIW Berlin 1115, DIW Berlin.

Buccellato, T. (2007). Convergence across russian regions: A spatial econometrics approach. Working Paper N 72, CEFIMS.

Canuto, O. and Cavallari, M. (2012). Natural Capital and the Resource Curse. *World Bank - Economic Premise, The World Bank*, (83):1–6.

Carmichael, F. (2005). *A Guide to Game Theory*. Harlow: Pearson Education.

Cass, D. (1965). Optimum growth in an aggregative model of capital accumulation. *Review of Economic Studies*, 32:233–240.

Cavalcanti, T. V., Mohaddes, K., and Raissi, M. (2009). Growth, development and natural resources: New evidence using a heterogeneous panel analysis. Cambridge Working Papers in Economics 0946, Faculty of Economics.

Chao, J. C., Hausman, J. A., Newey, W. K., Swanson, N. R., and Woutersen, T. (2014). Testing overidentifying restrictions with many instruments and heteroskedasticity. *Journal of Econometrics*, 178(P1):15–21.

Clarke, S. (2002). Market and institutional determinants of wage differentiation in russia. *Industrial and Labor Relations Review*, 55(4):pp. 628–648.

Congleton, R. D. (2004). The median voter model. In Rowley, C. K. and Schneider, F., editors, *The Encyclopedia of Public Choice*, pages 707–712. Dordrecht: Kluwer Academic Publishers.

Cornes, R. and Sandler, T. (1986). *The Theory of Externalities, Public Goods and Club Goods*. Cambridge: Cambridge University Press.

Costinot, A. and Donaldson, D. (2012). Ricardo's Theory of Comparative Advantage: Old Idea, New Evidence. *American Economic Review*, 102(3):453–458.

De Rosa, D. and Iootty, M. (2012). Are natural resources cursed? an investigation of the dynamic effects of resource dependence on institutional quality. Working Paper N. 6151, World Bank.

Dobler, C. and Hagemann, H. (2011). Economic growth in the post-socialist Russian Federation after 1991: The role of Institutions. Working Paper N. 34/2011, Violette Reihe Arbeitspapiere.

Downs, A. (1957). An Economic Theory of Political Action in a Democracy. *Journal of Political Economy*, 65:135–150.

Drobyshevsky, S., Lugovoy, O., Astafyeva, E., Polevoy, D., Kozlovskaya, A., Trunin, P., and Lederman, L. (2005). *Factors of Economic Growth in Russia's Regions*. Moscow: Gaidar Institute for Economic Policy.

Eberhardt, M. and Teal, F. (2013). Structural change and cross-country growth empirics. Working Paper N. 6335, World Bank.

Firdaus, M. and Yosup, Z. (2009). Dynamic analysis of regional convergence in indonesia. *Int. Journal of Economics and Management*, 3(1):73–86.

Gathmann, M. and Koch, R. (2013). Auf Rubel komm raus. *duzMAGAZIN*, 02/13. Available at: http://www.duz.de/duz-magazin/2013/02.

Gluschenko, K. (2010). Methodologies of Analyzing Inter-Regional Income Inequality and Their Applications to Russia. Working Paper N. 984, William Davidson Institute.

Guriev, S. and Rachinsky, A. (2005). The Role of Oligarchs in Russian Capitalism. *Journal of Economic Perspectives*, 19(1):131–150.

Guriev, S. and Vakulenko, E. (2012). Convergence between Russian regions. Working Paper N. w0180, Center for Economic and Financial Research (CEFIR).

Gylfason, T. (2001). Natural Resources and Economic Growth: What Is the Connection? Working Paper N. 530, CESifo Group Munich.

Habakkuk, H. (1962). *American and British technology in the nineteenth century*. Cambridge: Cambridge University Press.

Hagemann, H. (2009). Solow's 1956 Contribution to the Harrod-Domar Model. *History of Political Economy*, 41(Suppl. (1)):67–87.

Hagemann, H. (2010). Wassily Leontief and his German period. Available at: http://www.eshet.net/conference/paper_view.php?id=617&p=28.

Hamilton, J. (1994). *Time series*. Princeton: Princeton University Press.

Harrod, R. F. (1939). An essay in dynamic theory. *The Economic Journal*, 49(193):14–33.

Heckman, J. J., Lochner, L., and Todd, P. (2005). Earnings functions, rates of return and treatment effects: The mincer equation and beyond. Discussion Paper N. 1700, Institute for the Study of Labor Discussion Papers.

Hedlund, S. (2005). *Russian Path Dependence*. New York: Routledge.

Hedlund, S. (2008). Such a beautiful dream: How russia did not become a market economy. *The Russian Review*, 67(2):187–208.

Hoff, K. and Stiglitz, J. E. (2004). After the Big Bang? Obstacles to the Emergence of the Rule of Law in Post-Communist Societies. *American Economic Review*, 94(3):753–763.

Hotelling, H. (1929). Stability in competition. *The Economic Journal*, 39:41–57.

Hsiao, C. (1981). Autoregressive modelling and money-income causality detection. *Journal of Monetary Economics*, 7(1):85–106.

Islam, N. (1995). Growth Empirics: A Panel Data Approach. *The Quarterly Journal of Economics*, 110(4):1127–1170.

Kar, D. and Freitas, S. (2013). Russia: Illicit financial flows and the role of the underground economy. Global Financial Integrity Report.

Knox, Z. and Mitrofanova, A. (2014). Eastern christianity and politics in the twenty-first century. In *The Russian Orthodox Church*, pages 38–67. New York: Routledge.

Koopmans, T. (1965). On the concept of optimal economic growth. In *Study Week on the Econometric Approach to Development Planning, N. 28*, pages 225–287. Vatican: Pontificae Academia Scientiarum.

Koritzky, A. (2010). *Human capital as a factor of regional economic growth in Russia [Chelovecheski kapital kak faktor ekonomicheskogo rosta regionov Rossii]*. Novosibirsk: Siberian University of Consumer's Cooperation.

Kufenko, V. (2012). Empirical analysis of regional economic performance in russia: Human capital perspective. Working Paper N. 38/2012, Violette Reihe Arbeitspapiere.

Kutner, M., Nachtsheim, C., and Neter, J. (2004). *Applied Linear Regression Models*. New York: McGraw-Hill/Irwin, 4th edition.

Kuznets, S. (1955). Economic Growth and Income Inequality. *American Economic Review*, 65:1–28.

Ledyaeva, S. and Linden, M. (2008). Determinants of Economic Growth: Empirical Evidence from Russian Regions. *European Journal of Comparative Economics*, 5(1):87–105.

Leite, C. and Weidmann, J. (1999). Does Mother Nature Corrupt. Working Paper N. 99/85, International Monetary Fund.

Li, G. (1985). Robust regression. In *Exploring Data Tables, Trends, and Shapes*, pages 281–343. New York: Wiley.

Libman, A. (2012a). Democracy and Growth: Is The Effect Non-Linear? *Economic Research Guardian*, 2(1):99–120.

Libman, A. (2012b). Democracy, size of bureaucracy, and economic growth: evidence from Russian regions. *Empirical Economics*, 43(3):1321–1352.

Libman, A., Kozlov, V., and Schultz, A. (2012). Roving Bandits in Action: Outside Option and Governmental Predation in Autocracies. *Kyklos*, 65(4):526–562.

Lucas, R. J. (1988). On the mechanics of economic development. *Journal of Monetary Economics*, 22(1):3–42.

Luelfesmann, C. (2007). Dual Provision of Public Policies in Democracy. Working Paper N. dp07-20, Simon Fraser University.

Mankiw, N. G., Romer, D., and Weil, D. N. (1992). A Contribution to the Empirics of Economic Growth. *The Quarterly Journal of Economics*, 107(2):407–437.

Manukyan, A. (2011). *Fraudulent Elections, Political Protests, and Regime Transitions*. PhD thesis, Georgia State University. Available at: http://scholarworks.gsu.edu/political_science_diss/21/.

McGuire, M. C. and Olson, M. (1996). The Economics of Autocracy and Majority Rule: The Invisible Hand and the Use of Force. *Journal of Economic Literature*, 34(1):72–96.

Melnikov, R. (2005). Analysis of the dynamics of inter-regional economic inequality: foreign approaches and the russian practice. *Region: Economics and Sociology [Region: Ekonomika i Sotsiologia]*, 4:3–18.

Mikheeva, N. (1999). Analysis of interregional inequality in russia. *Studies on Russian Economic Development*, 10(5):514–521.

Mincer, J. (1958). Investment in Human Capital and Personal Income Distribution. *Journal of Political Economy*, 66:281–302.

Mo, P. H. (2001). Corruption and Economic Growth. *Journal of Comparative Economics*, 29(1):66–79.

Montgomery, D. C., Jennings, C. L., and Kulahci, M. (2008). *Introduction to Time Series Analysis and Forecasting*. Hoboken: John Wiley & Sons, Inc. (Wiley).

Nelson, R. R. and Phelps, E. S. (1966). Investment in humans, technological diffusion, and economic growth. *The American Economic Review*, 56(1/2):69–75.

North, D. C. (1990). *Institutions, Institutional Change and Economic Performance*. Cambridge: Cambridge University Press.

Obrien, R. (2007). A caution regarding rules of thumb for variance inflation factors. *Quality & Quantity: International Journal of Methodology*, 41(5):673–690.

Pashinova, T. and Strasky, J. (2012). What drives fdi to russian regions? Research Briefing, Deutsche Bank, DB Research.

Ramsey, F. (1928). A mathematical theory of saving. *Economic Journal*, 38(152):543–559.

Ramsey, J. B. (1969). Tests for specification errors in classical linear least squares regression analysis. *Journal of the Royal Statistical Society, Series B.*, 31(2):350–371.

Remington, T. (2011). *The Politics of Inequality in Russia*. Cambridge: Cambridge University Press.

Romer, P. M. (1994a). New goods, old theory, and the welfare costs of trade restrictions. *Journal of Development Economics*, 43(1):5–38.

Romer, P. M. (1994b). The Origins of Endogenous Growth. *Journal of Economic Perspectives*, 8(1):3–22.

Roodman, D. (2006). How to Do xtabond2: An introduction to difference and system GMM in Stata. Working Paper N. 103, Center for Global Development.

Rybczynski, T. M. (1955). Factor endowment and relative commodity prices. *Economica (New Series)*, 22(88):336–341.

Sachs, J. D. and Warner, A. M. (1995). Natural Resource Abundance and Economic Growth. Working Paper N. 5398, National Bureau of Economic Research, Inc.

Sachs, J. D. and Warner, A. M. (1997). Sources of Slow Growth in African Economies. *Journal of African Economies*, 6(3):335–376.

Sachs, J. D. and Warner, A. M. (2001). The curse of natural resources. *European Economic Review*, 45(4-6):827–838.

Sala-i-Martin, X. (1994). Cross-sectional regressions and the empirics of economic growth. *European Economic Review*, 38(3-4):739–747.

Sala-i-Martin, X. (1996). Regional cohesion: Evidence and theories of regional growth and convergence. *European Economic Review*, 40(6):1325–1352.

Sala-i-Martin, X. (1997). I Just Ran Two Million Regressions. *American Economic Review*, 87(2):178–183.

Sala-i-Martin, X. and Subramanian, A. (2013). Addressing the natural resource curse: An illustration from Nigeria. *Journal of African Economies*, 22(4):570–615.

Scervini, F. (2012). Empirics of the median voter: democracy, redistribution and the role of the middle class. *Journal of Economic Inequality*, 10(4):529–550.

Schultz, T. (1961). Investment in human capital. *American Economic Review*, 51(1):1–17.

Shleifer, A. and Vishny, R. W. (1993). Corruption. *The Quarterly Journal of Economics*, 108(3):599–617.

Sobolev, A. (2012). Factors of collective action: mass protests in russia in 2011-2012 [faktoru kollektivnogo deistvia: sluchai massovuch protestov v rossii 2011-2012]. Working Paper N. WP1/2012/05, Higher School of Economics.

Solanko, L. (2003). An empirical note on growth and convergence across Russian regions. Working Paper N. 9/2003, Bank of Finland.

Solow, R. (1952). On the structure of linear models. *Econometrica*, 20(1):29–46.

Solow, R. (1953). A note on the price level and interest rate in a growth model. *The Review of Economic Studies*, 21(1):74–79.

Solow, R. M. (1956). A contribution to the theory of economic growth. *The Quarterly Journal of Economics*, 70(1):65–94.

Swan, T. (1956). Economic growth and capital accumulation. *The Economic Record*, 32(2):334–361.

Tam, H. (2008). An economic or political Kuznets curve? *Public Choice*, 134(3):367–389.

Tinbergen, J. (1942). Zur theorie der langfristigen wirtschaftsentwicklung. *Weltwirtschaftliches Archiv*, 55:511–549.

Torvik, R. (2002). Natural resources, rent seeking and welfare. *Journal of Development Economics*, 67(2):455–470.

Tsybakov, A. (2009). *Introduction to Nonparametric Estimation*. New York: Springer Science+Business Media.

Ugur, M. and Dasgupta, N. (2011). Corruption and economic growth: A meta-analysis of the evidence on low-income countries and beyond. Working Paper N. 31226, University of Greenwich.

Uzawa, H. (1965). Optimum technical change in an aggregative model of economic growth. *International Economic Review*, 6(1):pp. 18–31.

Verardi, V. and Croux, C. (2009). Robust regression in stata. *Stata Journal*, 9(3):439–453.

Windmeijer, F. (2005). A finite sample correction for the variance of linear efficient two-step GMM estimators. *Journal of Econometrics*, 126(1):25–51.

Winer, S. L. and Hettich, W. (2004). The political economy of taxation: Positive and normative analysis when collective choice matters. In *The Encyclopedia of Public Choice*, pages 173–190. Dordrecht: Kluwer Academic Publishers.

Wood, A. and Berge, K. (1997). Exporting manufactures: Human resources, natural resources, and trade policy. *Journal of Development Studies*, 34(1):35–59.

Wooldridge, J. (2002). *Econometric Analysis of Cross Section and Panel Data*. Cambridge, MA: MIT Press, 2nd. edition.

Wu, A. (2007). An analysis of employee investment in specific human capital based on game theory. *Journal of Contemporary Management Issues*, 12(2):41–56.

Young, A. T., Higgins, M. J., and Levy, D. (2008). Sigma Convergence versus Beta Convergence: Evidence from U.S. County-Level Data. *Journal of Money, Credit and Banking*, 40(5):1083–1093.

6

Appendix

Fig. 20. Outliers for specification (12.2), Chapter 1

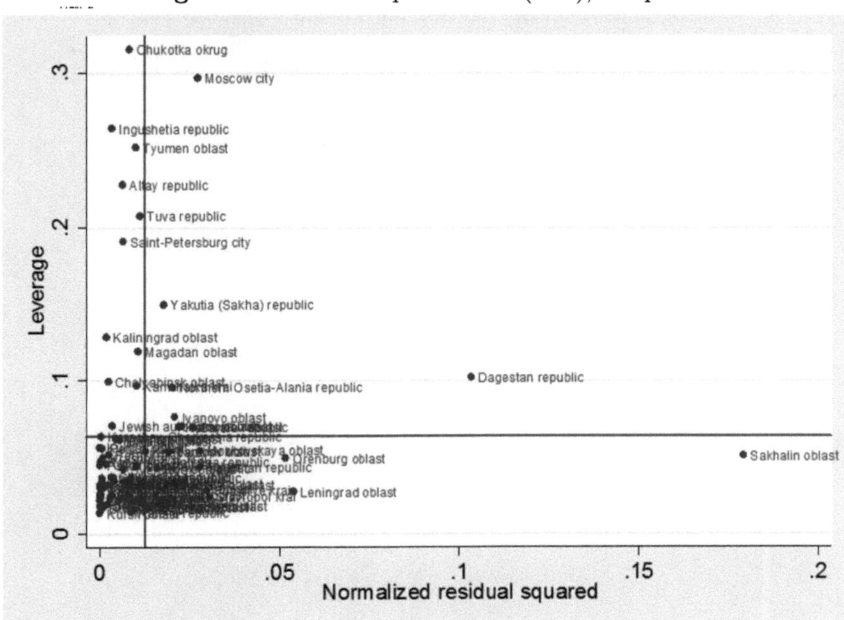

Data: Goskomstat

Fig. 21. Outliers for specification (12.5), Chapter 1

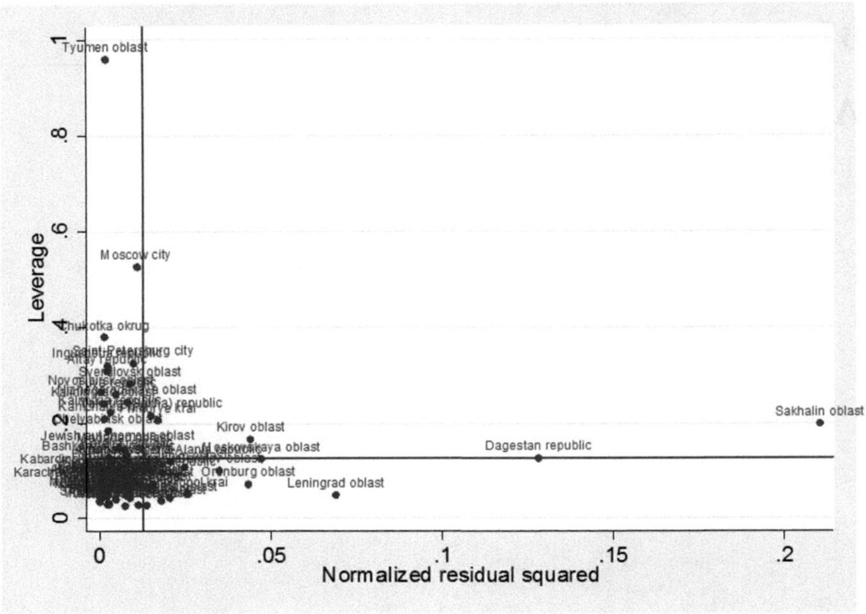

Data: Goskomstat

Fig. 22. Outliers for specification (32.1), Chapter 3

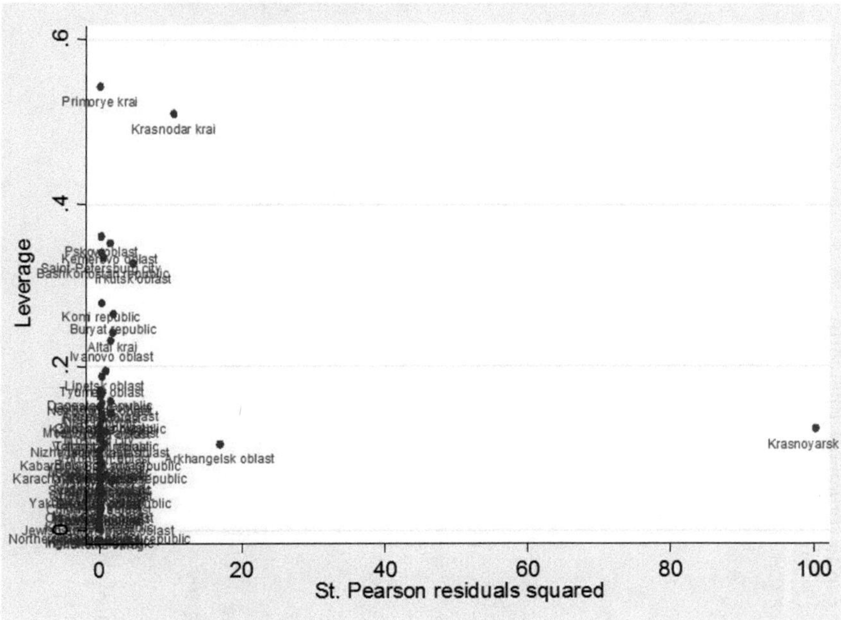

Data: Goskomstat

Fig. 23. Regional real GRP per capita dynamics 1995-2010

Data: Goskomstat

Table 12. Tests for model (13.2), Chapter 1

Arellano-Bond test for AR(2)	
Z stat.	0.33
Pr > Z	0.743
Sargan test of overid. restrictions	
Chi2 stat.	53.23
Pr > chi2	0.051
Hansen test of overid. restrictions	
Chi2 stat.	42.97
Pr > chi2	0.267
Difference-in-Hansen tests of exogeneity of instrument subsets	
GMM instruments for levels	
Hansen test excluding group	
Chi2 stat.	39.28
Pr > chi2	0.245
Difference (H_0 = exogenous)	
Chi2 stat.	3.69
Pr > chi2	0.45
Standard instruments	
Hansen test excluding group	
Chi2 stat.	42.37
Pr > chi2	0.215
Difference (H_0 = exogenous)	
Chi2 stat.	0.61
Pr > chi2	0.739

Source: proprietary

Table 13. Tests for model (13.3), Chapter 1

	Arellano-Bond test for AR(2)
Z stat.	-0.58
Pr > Z	0.562
	Sargan test of overid. restrictions
Chi2 stat.	45.06
Pr > chi2	0.17
	Hansen test of overid. restrictions
Chi2 stat.	34.63
Pr > chi2	0.581
Difference-in-Hansen tests of exogeneity of instrument subsets	
	GMM instruments for levels
	Hansen test excluding group
Chi2 stat.	26.42
Pr > chi2	0.785
	Difference (H_0 = exogenous)
Chi2 stat.	8.21
Pr > chi2	0.084
	Standard instruments
	Hansen test excluding group
Chi2 stat.	28.09
Pr > chi2	0.616
	Difference (H_0 = exogenous)
Chi2 stat.	6.53
Pr > chi2	0.366

Source: proprietary

Table 14. List of regions (Goskomstat order)

Code	Region	Code	Region
1	the Belgorod oblast	41	the Rostov oblast
2	the Bryansk oblast	42	the Bashkortostan republic
3	the Vladimir oblast	43	the Mari El republic
4	the Voronezh oblast	44	the Mordovia republic
5	the Ivanovo oblast	45	the Tatarstan republic
6	the Kaluga oblast	46	the Udmurt republic
7	the Kostroma oblast	47	the Chuvashia republic
8	the Kursk oblast	48	the Perm krai
9	the Lipetsk oblast	49	the Kirov oblast
10	the Moskovskaya oblast	50	the Nizhegorodskaya oblast
11	the Orlovskaya oblast	51	the Orenburg oblast
12	the Ryazan oblast	52	the Penza oblast
13	the Smolensk oblast	53	the Samara oblast
14	the Tambov oblast	54	the Saratov oblast
15	the Tver oblast	55	the Ulyanovsk oblast
16	the Tula oblast	56	the Kurgan oblast
17	the Yaroslavl oblast	57	the Sverdlovsk oblast
18	Moscow city	58	the Tyumen oblast
19	the Karelia republic	59	the Chelyabinsk oblast
20	the Komi republic	60	the Altay republic
21	the Arkhangelsk oblast	61	the Buryat republic
22	the Vologda oblast	62	the Tuva republic
23	the Kaliningrad oblast	63	the Khakassia republic
24	the Leningrad oblast	64	the Altai krai
25	the Murmansk oblast	65	the Krasnoyarsk krai
26	the Novgorod oblast	66	the Irkutsk oblast
27	the Pskov oblast	67	the Kemerovo oblast
28	Saint-Petersburg city	68	the Novosibirsk oblast
29	the Adygeya republic	69	the Omsk oblast
30	the Dagestan republic	70	the Tomsk oblast
31	the Ingushetia republic	71	the Chitinskaya oblast
32	the Kabardino-Balkaria republic	72	the Yakutia (Sakha) republic
33	the Kalmykia republic	73	the Kamchatka krai
34	the Karachay-Cherkessia republic	74	the Primorye krai
35	the Northern Osetia-Alania republic	75	the Khabarovsk krai
36	the Chechnya republic	76	the Amur oblast
37	the Krasnodar krai	77	the Magadan oblast
38	the Stavropol krai	78	the Sakhalin oblast
39	the Astrakhan oblast	79	the Jewish autonomous oblast
40	the Volgograd oblast	80	the Chukotka okrug

Nomenclature

Chapter 1 - Neo-classical growth model

$1-u(t)$	Effort to accumulate human capital
$A(t)$	Efficiency parameter
g	Growth rate of technology or technological change
$H(t)$	Human capital
$K(t)$	Physical capital
$k(t)$	Capital-labour ratio
$L(t)$	Labour
n	Growth rate of population
s	Savings rate applied to output
$u(t)$	Non-leisure time used for production
$w(h)$	Technology adoption lag
$Y(t)$	Output
$y(t)$	Output per capita
α	Elasticity
β	Beta
δ	Depreciation rate
δ_h	Hypothetical human capital depreciation rate
$\dot{h}(t)$	Change of human capital
$\dot{k}(t)$	Change of physical capital in time
ψ	Human capital accumulation growth rate
σ	Sigma
c^*	Steady state consumption
$f'(k_{gold})_{RCK}$	The "golden level" of physical capital-labour ratio in the Ramsey-Cass-Koopmans model
$f'(k_{gold})_{Solow}$	The "golden level" of physical capital-labour in the Solow model
k^*	Steady state of the capital-labour ratio
p	Competitive rate of interest
s_h	Fraction of income invested in human capital
$Tech$	Theoretical level of technology

Chapter 1 - OLS growth regressions

α Constant
$\bar{x}_{i,t0,t1}$ Vector of control variables, averaged for the first two years
βs Coefficients
$\ln(y_{i,T}/y_{i,t=0})/T$ Average annual growth rate
T Time span
$u_{i,t}$ Error
$x_{i,T-t}$ Vector of variables for intermediate years during $T-t$
$y_{i,t=0}$ Level of initial income
$z_{i,T-t}$ Vector of controls including constant variables

Chapter 1 - System GMM estimation

βs Coefficients
$\Delta\hat{x}_{i,t}$ Vector of growth rates of control variables (endogenous)
$\Delta y_{i,t}$ Current growth rate of real GRP per capita
λ Speed of convergence (notation also used in Chpters 2 and 3)
$d_{i,t}$ Vector of period or year dummies (exogenous)
e Mathematical constant
$E_{i,t}$ Composite error term: specific and idiosyncratic errors
T Time span
$\hat{y}_{i,t-1}$ Lagged level of GRP per capita (endogenous)

Chapter 2 - Game theory

Δ Change condition (Switching rule)
λ Pecuniary reward for staying
π Rate of return to investment in terms of human capital
C Payoff for changing
HC Present level of human capital
I Investment in human capital
k Non-pecuniary reward for changing
n Non-pecuniary reward for staying
$p; (1-p)$ Probability
p^* Critical probability
v Rate of diminution of human capital
V^{ignore} Expected utility of ignoring the investment opportunity
V^{invest} Expected utility of investing
w Current real wage
z Pecuniary reward for changing

Chapter 3 - The Political Kuznets curve

$1-\delta$ Share of the poor population
$1-\mu_{cost}$ Fraction of wealth which would remain after the revolution (in R_2, notation changed)
$1-\mu_{remain}$ Fraction of wealth which would be destroyed after the revolution (in R_1, notation changed)
β Coefficient
δ Share of the rich population
γ Savings rate
λ Share of the poor economic agents
μ_{cost} Cost of the revolution (in R_2, notation changed)

μ_{remain}	Fraction of wealth which would remain after the revolution (in R_1, notation changed)
$\overline{y}$	Average income
A	Efficiency parameter
h_t^p	Human capital level of the poor
h_t^r	Human capital level of the rich
h_t	Human capital level
h_{ss}	Steady state level of human capital
R_1	Constraint 1 (if holds, no revolution is expected)
R_2	Constraint 2 (if holds, a revolution can occur)
Y_{ss}^1	Steady state of the income (autocracy, if only the rich accumulate)
Y_{ss}^2	Steady state of the income (autocracy, both the poor and the rich accumulate)
Y_{ss}^3	Steady state of the income (democracy, both the poor and the rich accumulate under certain conditions)
y_t^p	Income of the poor population
y_t^r	Income of the rich population
Z	Offspring's initial level of human capital

Chapter 3 - Logistic model

βs	Coefficients
$\partial y/\partial x$	Marginal effect, at means
ϑ	Latent variable
$protest_i$	Binary variable
u_i	Error
Z_i	Additional controls

Abbreviations

CBR	Central Bank of Russia
CIA	Central Intelligence Agency
CPI	Consumer Price Index
FD	First Differences
FDI	Foreign Direct Investment
GDP	Gross Domestic Product
GMM	Generalized Method of Moments
GNP	Gross National Product
Goskomstat	Russian Federal State Statistics Service
GRP	Gross Regional Product
MVT	Median Voter Theorem
N	Number of cases (panels)
OECD	Organization for Economic Cooperation and Development
OLS	Ordinary Least Squares
OV Test	Ramsey specification test (omitted variable test)
RBC	Russian Business Consulting
T	Time period(s)
VIF	Variance Inflation Factor
WCIOM	Russian Public Opinion Research Center
WG	Within Group estimator

MIX
Papier aus verantwortungsvollen Quellen
Paper from responsible sources
FSC® C105338

If you have any concerns about our products,
you can contact us on
ProductSafety@springernature.com

In case Publisher is established outside the EU,
the EU authorized representative is:
Springer Nature Customer Service Center GmbH
Europaplatz 3, 69115 Heidelberg, Germany

Printed by Libri Plureos GmbH
in Hamburg, Germany